"Rabbi Shoshana Hantman has done something extraordinary with this collection of Passover parodies: she's written pitch-perfect versions of many familiar icons of North American culture, conspiring with their fictional characters to teach the story, symbols, and meaning(s) of Passover and its rituals. It's a wildly funny, witty, and entertaining fusion of stand-up comedy, slapstick reinvention, and powerful messages. I can't remember anyone ever doing this in quite this way and with such panache! It's destined to become a Passover tradition!"

— Rabbi Larry Pinsker, Congregation Beit Tikvah, Baltimore, Maryland

"Parody, or in Yiddish, *machen choyzek*, of even the most sacred traditions has a long and honorable history in Judaism. Shoshana Hantman's *Passover Parodies* gently and lovingly brings *choyzek* to the celebration of Passover, arguably the festival most widely celebrated by American Jews of all persuasions. *Passover Parodies* is guaranteed to enliven any seder."

— Dr. S. David Sperling, Professor of Bible, Hebrew Union College–Jewish Institute of Religion

"If you don't think already that Passover is a happy holiday, *Passover Parodies* will change your mind. Another glass of wine wouldn't hurt either."

— Arnold Roth, cartoonist, *Punch, The New Yorker, Playboy*

PASSOVER PARODIES

Passover Parodies:

Short Plays for the Seder Table

Shoshana Hantman

Sidney Books

NEW YORK

www.passoverparodies.com

To contact the author, write to RabbiHantman@passoverparodies.com

Cover design: Christina Mattison (www.cmattison.com)
Interior typeface: Book Antiqua
Cover typefaces: OptimusPrinceps, Black Jack, and Bernhard Modern
Standard

ISBN: 978-0-9913512-2-0

First Sidney Books trade paperback edition February 2014

10 9 8 7 6 5 4 3 2 1

This book is dedicated to the memory of my father,
Sidney G. Hantman
who taught me to write,

and to the memory of my mother,
Sylvia W. Hantman,
who taught me to explore,

and is also dedicated to my husband,
Richard E. Weill
who has made it possible for me to do both.

ACKNOWLEDGMENTS

Many friends and relatives have supported the creation of this book. Foremost among them is my dear husband Richard Weill, who not only supplied the gift of time, but also is a valuable creative, academic and legal resource. Rich's well-trained eye and ear were essential. There would be no book without him.

Next is my friend and neighbor Dr. Joel M. Hoffman, a prolific author, who supplied essential help with website creation and other aspects of book promotion. I doubt I would have had the nerve to try this without Joel's encouragement.

Others have read the manuscript and offered feedback. They include Amy Hersh, Cheryl Jagow, Rabbi Ivan Caine, Rabbi Jennifer Jaech, Maureen O'Shea, Michael Kannen, Maria Lambros, Sandra Mamis, Barbara Spackman, Mike Miller, Gail Brussel, NoaSapir Franklin, and dozens of members of my professional alliance, the Reconstructionist Rabbinical Association. I am grateful for their enthusiasm. At least, I *think* it was enthusiasm.

For twenty years, the students of the Halutsim Hebrew School have been reading my scripts in class, and proving that even comic readings are effective promoters of creative thinking and communal reflection. I cannot thank them all by name, but they know who they are.

Christina Mattison's artistic talent and good judgment have provided me with a very beautiful cover, and I thank her.

My children, Mollie and Isaac Hantman-Weill, have usually been patient with their mother's preoccupation, and have supplied the occasional idea or rhyme that I needed.

I should not leave out Clement Wood (1888-1950) and Dr. Peter Mark Roget (1779-1869). They wrote the rhyming dictionary and the thesaurus that now lie in tatters from over-use. Gentlemen, your work is an eternal blessing.

February 2014

CONTENTS

Introduction

The seder is, essentially, a symposium. That's what the rabbis who invented it during the ascendancy of the Greek empire envisioned. There was a lot to like in Greek culture (something rarely mentioned in the Hanukkah story), and the tradition of a group of philosophers sitting around a wine-laden table, discussing the nature of liberation and the responsibilities of freedom, was among its best features. We Jews knew we could do great things with this.

And so the springtime lamb sacrifice was ended, though a shank-bone remained as a memorial, and the symposium was instituted. "The more one expounds upon the Exodus, the more one is to be praised," wrote the seder's creators, and they put in four good questions to launch the discussion. The ancient rabbis didn't want this festive event to end the way they thought Greek symposia usually did ('symposium' means 'drinking together'), so they limited the imbibing to four cups of wine. But make no mistake, the seder is very Greek. We still keep some Hellenic names in it, like karpas and afikomen. Cultural borrowing is a universal phenomenon. When we take someone else's traditional content and re-shape it using our own ideals, that's revaluation. It enriches our culture.

Themes and references of the Torah's Exodus story are found in Western literature and other social forms. As I began seeing them, I realized I could zoom in to aspects of modern cultural expressions and highlight through parody their use of Biblical elements.

It's possible to conduct a seder simply by reading through the haggadah. There are some wonderful haggadot out there, and you can learn a lot. But the true spirit of this unique religious celebration is served by contributing your own voice, and to assist you, I have written these short plays. They are inspired by the traditional Purim parody, or *shpiel*, which has been a Jewish satirical outlet for centuries. If *shpiels* are fun on Purim, they'll be fun

1

on Passover, but more important, they will stimulate new discussions, new ideas, and new creativity.

This is important: no individual or family is expected to be interested in *all* these plays. There's a wide variety of subjects, and some will attract you more than others. The idea is to pick one you like. Maybe you'll choose a different one next year. Maybe there's one the kids like, and they can perform it for the group. Or, perhaps, you always wanted to be Groucho Marx, Sherlock Holmes, or Little Buttercup yourself.

My hope is that the *shpiels* will be useful, that they will help seder participants of all ages focus on some of the intriguing, astonishing, amusing and uplifting aspects of the Passover celebration.

UNDERSTANDING THE PASSOVER REFERENCES IN THESE PLAYS

The springtime festival of Passover – *Pesah* in Hebrew – is a festival of freedom. Its historical pretext is the exodus of the ancient Hebrews from slavery in Egypt, about 1250 B.C.E. This celebration was added to an even older pagan holiday, a festival of unleavened bread. The Passover we celebrate today is a hybrid of both. It now underscores our obligation to resist tyranny everywhere, in pursuit of the Biblical commandment, "You shall be a holy people, for I the Lord am holy."

The signature observance of Passover is the seder, a home ritual that includes traditional readings, prayers, song, rituals, and a meal. The seder takes place on the evening of the first full moon after the spring equinox; its Hebrew date is the fifteenth day of the month of Nisan. Many Jewish families outside of Israel conduct *two* seders, on the first two nights of the holiday.

For the entire eight days of Passover (for some families, seven), Jews eat no leavened products – bread, pasta, cakes, cereal, cookies, crackers, beer or grain alcohol. There are substitutes available for many of these, which often are made from potato flour, but they're generally abominable.

All the words of the seder ritual are contained in a book called the haggadah, or 'telling'; it exists in hundreds of different editions to suit every community. Usually, each participant has his or her own haggadah. On the table, in addition to all the normal acoutrements of a festive dinner, are a special wineglass for the prophet Elijah (the invisible guest at every seder), bowls of salt water representing the tears of the slaves, horseradish, green vegetables, a plate bearing three sheets of matza, an apple-and-nut mix called haroset, and a special seder plate.

On the seder plate are a number of symbolic items. A roasted egg represents the daily sacrifice in the Temple in Jerusalem; a lamb shankbone, the Passover sacrifice; a bitter vegetable like horseradish, the bitterness of oppression; a green such as parsley, the renewal of springtime; and a sample of the haroset, the brick and mortar which were the slave's daily lot.

The seder begins with the lighting of festival candles, the blessing of the holiday with wine (the Kiddush), the washing of hands, dipping parsley in salt water, the presentation of the matza with the declaration "may all who are hungry come and eat." A piece of matza called the afikomen is set aside; it will be the last bite eaten. (This rule was originally intended to limit the drinking.)

All this takes place as participants recline, or at least have pillows on their chairs. Reclining was understood to be mealtime custom of free people when the seder originated.

The four questions, asked by the youngest child present, launches the telling of the Exodus story, or 'maggeed.' During the story, the song *Dayenu* ("it would have been enough for us") is sung. Then come the two matza blessings, the eating of the bitter herb, and finally the meal is eaten, ending with the afikomen. The children by this point will have either surrendered the stolen afikomen for a prize, or found its hiding place.

The door is opened and the prophet Elijah invited in. Grace after the meal *(birkat ha-mazon)* follows, then Biblical psalms of praise, and several well-loved songs including <u>H</u>ad Gadya, E<u>h</u>ad Mee Yodea, and Adir Hu. The seder concludes with the wish, "Next year in Jerusalem."

Play It Again, Moses

— a Casablanca play —

Casablanca is a World War II version of the Exodus story. The film, adapted by Jewish writers Howard Koch and Julius and Philip Epstein from an unproduced play, is about a reluctant hero who is cajoled into helping subjugated freedom-fighters escape their oppressor. He has guarded his neutrality, but eventually, through his actions and the risks he takes, makes clear his dedication to the cause of the tyrant's victims. It's a very convincing description of the Pharaoh's adopted grandson, Moses. Rick Blaine's unexpected reunion with an old acquaintance, Ilsa's anguished uncertainty about whether to go or stay, and even the powerful instrument of freedom in the form of the letters of transit – all these have parallels in the Biblical story.

In *Play It Again, Moses*, Moses, Miriam, Aaron and Lotus Ra have the most substantial parts; Cartouche, the Pharaoh and the Narrator have fewer lines. Miriam has a song to sing. If she doesn't want to, Aaron could sing it instead. Or, everyone could.

NARRATOR
MOSES
LOTUS RA
MIRIAM
PHARAOH
AARON
CARTOUCHE

NARRATOR   Hebrew slaves – descended from the sons of Jacob who fled famine in their native land.   From the Chaldees to the Jordan Valley – across the Sinai to Goshen in Egypt.   Here, the fortunate ones, through money — or influence – or luck – obtain exit visas and scurry to Midian. But there are very few lucky ones. The others wait in Goshen – and wait – and wait –

We find an interesting group of people gathered in Moses' Café, just outside Goshen.

LOTUS RA   What on earth's going on there?

CARTOUCHE   An Egyptian taskmaster was found murdered in the desert. Too bad, eh?

MOSES   He got a break. Yesterday he was just an Egyptian taskmaster; today he's the Honored Dead.

CARTOUCHE   You will forgive me for saying this, M'sieur Moses, but you are a very cynical person.

MOSES   I forgive you.

LOTUS RA   Moses, I have often speculated on why you do not return to the Promised Land. Did you meet a pagan priest's daughter? Did you see a burning bush? I like to think that you killed a man. It is the romantic in me.

MOSES   It was a combination of all three.

LOTUS RA	And what in heaven's name brought you to Midian?
MOSES	My health. I came to Midian to tend sheep.
LOTUS RA	Sheep? What sheep? We're in a bar.
MOSES	I was misinformed.
NARRATOR	In walks the arrogant and cruel Pharaoh Strasser.
LOTUS RA	Ah, Pharaoh Strasser! Unoccupied Goshen welcomes you to Egypt.
PHARAOH	Thank you, Captain, it's very good to be here. The murder of the taskmaster – what has been done?
LOTUS RA	We already know who the murderer is.
PHARAOH	Good. Is he in custody?
LOTUS RA	There is no hurry. Tonight he will come to Moses'. Everybody comes to Moses'.
CARTOUCHE	*(whispering)* Moses, it is said that the Egyptian taskmaster was carrying signs and wonders that could free the Hebrews from servitude. It is also said that you have those signs and wonders right here in your café. They could easily be used to get Pharaoh Strasser to free the Hebrew slaves.
NARRATOR	Suddenly, Lotus Ra catches sight of Miriam, who has just walked into the room.
LOTUS RA	Mademoiselle – I heard that you were the most beautiful woman ever to visit the Nile Valley. That is a gross understatement.
MIRIAM	You are very kind. Captain – the boy who's playing the timbrel – somewhere I have seen him.
LOTUS RA	Aaron? He came here from Midian with Moses.
MIRIAM	Moses? Who is he?

LOTUS RA   Mademoiselle, you are in Moses'.

NARRATOR   Moses enters the room. He sees Miriam. Miriam sees him.

LOTUS RA   Moses, my dear friend, may I have the honor of introducing –

MOSES   Hello, Miriam.

MIRIAM   Hello, Moses.

LOTUS RA   You know each other? As a matter of fact, I seem to detect a strong family resemblance.

MIRIAM   Let's see, the last time we met …

MOSES   It was in the bulrushes.

MIRIAM   How nice – you remembered. But of course – that was four hundred years after the Jews marched into Egypt.

MOSES   I remember every detail: the Egyptians wore skirts, you wore a tallis. But mostly I remember the wow finish. A guy in a basket, floating in the bulrushes, with a comical look on his face because he has a diaper that needs changing.

MIRIAM   Please don't. I can understand how you feel.

MOSES   You might tell me who it was you left me for.

MIRIAM   Moses – I'm a Hebrew slave. And I'm your sister. I know you were just a baby when we sent you away, but, Moses, you're a Hebrew too! Think back, Moses!

[Melody: "As Time Goes By"]

> *You must remember this*
> *The day you had your bris*
> *The whitefish and the rye!*
> *The moyl, I think, was uncle Sy!*

Please, Moses, try.

You've never been to shul,
Neurotic as a rule
Horseradish makes you cry –
You hanker after matza-brei,
And don't know why.

Cream cheese on bagels, not Camembert or Brie
You hear of a simcha, and want to plant a tree
In winter, Miami is where you want to be – it's nothing
                you deny.

From Chelm to Bora-Bora,
It's still the same old Torah
And you're the major guy!
The seder's not the same without you –
Please, Moses, try.

MOSES   I'm not interested in world events. I'm a shepherd.
         Politics are for grown-ups.

AARON   That wasn't always your attitude.

MOSES   Wasn't it?

AARON   My friends here in the slave-cabins tell me you
         have quite a record. You ran straw to the brick-
         yards. You fought for workers' rights. And now,
         you're in possession of powerful signs and won-
         ders. For example, your shepherd's staff, Moses – I
         believe it has the ability to change into a serpent.
         You should check it out.

MOSES   I check my stick out for nobody.

AARON   Would you accept an offer of a hundred thousand
         shekels for those signs and wonders?

MOSES   If you offered me a million shekels, my answer
         would still be no.

AARON   I don't understand. There must be some reason

	you won't use them to free the Hebrews.
MOSES	There is. I suggest you ask your sister.
AARON	She's your sister, too.
MIRIAM	Moses, I know how you feel about me, and I don't blame you. But I'm asking you to put your feelings aside for something more important. In your own way, you're fighting for the same thing – for the freedom of the Hebrews, so they can return to the Promised Land and become a light to the nations. You're our last hope. If you don't help us, Jewish history will end in Egypt.
MOSES	What of it? A lot of history is going to end in Egypt.
AARON	Moses, each of us has a destiny. I wonder if you know you're trying to escape from yourself and that you'll never succeed. The Hebrews are going to follow you wherever you go. That is what I mean by your destiny.

(Knock at the door.)

CARTOUCHE	Miriam and Aaron, you will come with us. We have a warrant to double your quota of bricks. You Hebrews are to produce them.
MIRIAM	But that's not humanly possible!
CARTOUCHE	You will all return to work under a safe conduct from Pharaoh Strasser.
MIRIAM	And of what value is that? You may recall what Egyptian guarantees have been worth in the past.
CARTOUCHE	Captain Ra will discuss that with you later.

(Aaron, Miriam and Cartouche exit.)

| MOSES | It seems 'destiny' has taken a hand. |

LOTUS RA	I would think that the Hebrews will remain slaves in Egypt for the foreseeable future.
MOSES	Your magicians haven't got the signs and wonders to keep them in slavery. You might as well let them go now.
LOTUS RA	Moses, I would advise you not to interest yourself too much in what happens to the Hebrews. If by any chance you were to help them escape –
MOSES	What makes you think I'm interested?
LOTUS RA	Because one: you are in possession of signs and wonders. Two: you bet me ten thousand shekels that the slaves would be freed. And three: you may do it just because you don't like Pharaoh's looks. As a matter of fact, I don't like them either. Too much makeup and he always walks sideways.
MOSES	Yes, they're all excellent reasons. But I'm using these signs and wonders myself – I'm borrowing my neighbors' jewelry, and leaving Goshen on tonight's camel – with my brother and sister. That ought to rest your fears about my helping the Hebrews escape.
LOTUS RA	But you don't have to tell me that. You have the signs and wonders. You can use them to leave with your family any time you please. Why do you care what happens to the rest of the Hebrews?
MOSES	I don't. Look, Lotus, if you could catch the Israelites trying to escape, and then triple their quota of bricks, would that be a feather in your cap?
LOTUS RA	It most certainly would. But why would you think Pharaoh cares about *you*?
MOSES	He doesn't. But Aaron is a talented magician. He knows a good deal that Pharaoh would like to know. If you let my people go, and be at my place

a half hour before the camel leaves, I'll arrange for the Israelites to sacrifice lambs, bake some matza and you'll have grounds to triple their workload, if you like. Pharaoh won't even notice I'm leaving with Miriam and Aaron. The problems of three little people don't amount to a hill of farfel to him.

LOTUS RA   Moses, I will miss you. Apparently you're the only one in Goshen that has even less scruples than I.

MOSES   Thanks. By the way, call off your watchdogs at the Red Sea. I don't want them around at midnight. I'm taking no chances, Lotus, even with you.

NARRATOR   Midnight finds the Hebrew slaves packed and ready to flee Egypt. The Egyptians have been plagued by a multitude of signs and wonders – among them, blood, frogs, lice, and cattle disease. Suddenly a great cry arose in Egypt.

PHARAOH   The first-born have all been struck dead! The Hebrews are leaving! Hello, hello – get me the radio tower! Send the army after the slaves – they're headed toward the Red Sea!

AARON   Moses, strike the water with your staff. The water will divide and we'll be able to run through it!

MIRIAM   But, do we really want to leave Egypt and cross the Red Sea, Moses? We don't know what's out there. There could be millions of acres of wilderness. Rebellions, enemies, questionable theology! I'm not sure I want to take this step. Maybe I should just go back and be a slave.

MOSES   Miriam, if you don't cross the Red Sea, you'll regret it. Maybe not today, maybe not tomorrow. But soon, and for millennia.

CARTOUCHE   The waters have divided! The Hebrews are running through to the other side!

MOSES	Come on, Miriam! Do you have any idea what we've got to look forward to in Egypt? Nine chances out of ten we'd end up entombed in a pyramid, holding a plate of olives for a mummy. We both know you belong with the Israelites. Who else could lead us in song at the other side of the Red Sea?
AARON	Moses, it's Lotus Ra!
MOSES	I'll hold him here until all the Israelites have gotten across.
NARRATOR	The Hebrews are crossing through the Red Sea on dry land – and with them, Miriam and Aaron.
AARON	Thank you for everything, Moses. And welcome back to the fight. This time, I know our side will win.
LOTUS RA	Moses, I was right. You *are* a sentimentalist.
MOSES	I don't know what you're talking about.
LOTUS RA	I suppose you know that this is not going to be pleasant for either of us ... especially for you. Pharaoh Strasser is almost here, and I'll have to arrest you, of course.
MOSES	When the Israelites have all passed through, Lotus.
PHARAOH	What is the meaning of this? Why are the slaves running through the sea? Men – go after them and bring them back!
MOSES	There are certain portions of the Red Sea, Pharaoh, that I wouldn't advise you to try to cross.
PHARAOH	Captain Ra, why do you stand there? Why don't you stop them?
LOTUS RA	Ask Moses.

PHARAOH   I would recommend that you not interfere with a Pharaoh of the Middle Bronze Age. Men, I will lead you after the Israelites myself!

NARRATOR   And the Pharaoh leads his army through the divided sea. At a signal from Moses, the waters come crashing back into place, drowning Pharaoh and his army.

CARTOUCHE   *(breathless)* Captain Ra! What has happened?

LOTUS RA   Pharaoh Strasser has been drowned. Round up the usual suspects.

MOSES   Thanks, Lotus.

LOTUS RA   Moses, until this affair dies down, it might be just as well for me to disappear from Egypt. I understand there's a Canaanite garrison up in the Judean hills. If you're interested, I could come along as your aide-de-camp.

MOSES   That's fine with me, Lotus. But it doesn't make any difference about our bet. You still owe me ten thousand shekels.

LOTUS RA   That can buy a lot of manna ... Moses, I think this is the beginning of a beautiful civilization.

The Sign of Four Questions

— a Sherlock Holmes play —

The Torah is jam-packed with mysteries.

The biggest one is its origin. In the nineteenth century, Bible scholars using literary analysis noticed several distinctive styles of writing, and were able to postulate four sources of the text that were eventually woven together. This was the documentary hypothesis, which is still undergoing investigation and refinement.

Feminist Biblical scholars have an additional puzzle to solve. Our ancestors' experience and religious philosophy were recorded by men. What would women have contributed to the sacred text, had they been able to add their voices? How would Jewish laws and traditions be different? This quest, too, requires a great deal of historical digging, as well as intuition.

Asking the questions of a detective – "What actually happened?" – means putting aside all assumptions and hearsay, and focusing entirely on facts. This is exceedingly difficult when we approach a subject with which we have an emotional relationship, like the Bible. The cold eye of Sherlock Holmes is really needed, if we want the truth.

For example, near the beginning of the shpiel, Dr. Watson mentions the curious ritual found in the book of Exodus, chapter four, verses 24 through 26. There, after an unclear but violent pursuit of, possibly, Moses, by Adonai, Moses' wife Tzipporah circumcises her son and utters a mysterious phrase. The liberation narrative then resumes without any explanation. The circumcision of infant Hebrews has always been a father's obligation, not a mother's. What could this mean? Was Tzipporah, a Midianite priest's daughter, enacting some forgotten ceremony which the Torah's editors, thousands of years ago, hesitated to clarify? Why did they bring it up at all?

That mystery is but one of thousands in the Bible, all of them tan-

15

talizing. But for the present moment, allow the world's greatest consulting detective to evaluate the evidence of the inedible dinner items, the marked door, the disappearing wine, the stolen afikomen, and the filtered fish.

Holmes has the major role, followed by Watson, Rebecca, and Mrs. Hudson.

WATSON
HOLMES
MRS. HUDSON
REBECCA

WATSON   Somewhere in the vaults of the British Museum, among the reams of ancient documents of the Hebrew people, there is a worn and battered dispatch-box with my name, John H. Watson, M.D., painted upon the lid. This box is crammed with my recollections of the cases of Mr. Sherlock Holmes which I had the privilege to observe. Some of these problems were complete failures, affording no final explanations, such as the conundrum of the red heifer in Numbers, chapter nineteen, in which a ritual of purification contaminates the officiant; this can hardly fail to annoy the casual reader. Others shall remain ever the private affairs of some of our most illustrious families, such as the case of Tzipporah's unexplained circumcision ritual, recorded without any solution in the fourth chapter of Exodus.

In other cases, however, I had a personal interest and can even speak as an eye-witness, and it is such an adventure that I essay to set forth here. My father was a wandering Aramean, and as we are enjoined to think of ourselves as personally redeemed from slavery in Egypt, I consider myself intimately concerned.

It was on a brisk spring afternoon when I returned home early from my rounds at Mt. Sinai, and found Holmes engaged in close examination of what appeared to be an odd bit of dry cracker.

Was luncheon so poorly presented, Holmes?

HOLMES   Your powers of deduction fail you, Watson. In fact, this strange comestible has come by today's post, accompanied by an urgent appeal from a young lady. Tell me, what does this cracker reveal about its owner's distress?

WATSON   Well, let's see. This appears to be quite dry, and completely perforated by a number of tiny holes. It's quite obvious that, having been left too long in a larder, this unfortunate piece of bread was the victim of a porcupine.

HOLMES   Watson, you never fail to astonish me with your vivid imagination. But I regret to discard your theory. The holes which you astutely observed are of a regular pattern. They were therefore not placed there by happenstance, but purposely inserted into the dough to hasten the baking process. Did you not note the complete absence of any leavening agent in this biscuit?

WATSON   I can't say that I did.

HOLMES   The cracker was produced by someone in a most urgent rush. Furthermore, it has been broken along one side. A segment has been removed.

WATSON   Why?

HOLMES   That is what we must endeavor to find out. In fact, that is essential to the request of the young person who sent it to me; she emphasizes that finding the other piece of this cracker is of the most vital importance. Here is the message she enclosed in the parcel.

WATSON   "Dear Mr. Holmes: I ask your help in finding the afikomen, which my parents have hidden somewhere in our house. Every year my brother finds it and I feel most strongly that it's my turn. It looks a lot like this piece of matza. If you need to ask any questions I'll come to call later today. Thank you ever so much – Rebecca Levy."

Why, it's just a children's game!

HOLMES	So it would seem. However, I have the impression that there's more to this than meets the eye. Have a look at this, Watson.
WATSON	It's a small volume in some foreign alphabet. I can make nothing of it.
HOLMES	It may be that our young friend can shed some light on this peculiar book. If I am not mistaken, here she is now.
MRS. HUDSON	Mr. Holmes, there's a Miss Levy to see you. Shall I show her in?
HOLMES	By all means.
REBECCA	How do you do, Mr. Holmes.
HOLMES	Fine, thank you, Miss Levy. Allow me to present Dr. Watson.
WATSON	A pleasure, I'm sure.
HOLMES	If you please, Miss Levy, state the facts as you recall them. Omit nothing.
REBECCA	Well, Mr. Holmes, every year at Passover, my parents have a seder at our house.
WATSON	What's that?
REBECCA	It's a special dinner when we re-tell the story of the Exodus from Egypt. My whole family comes: my grandparents, my aunts, my cousins, and my uncle Nigel.
HOLMES	Is there anything unusual about this seder?
REBECCA	There's something unusual about *every* seder.
HOLMES	Pray tell us.
REBECCA	They put vegetables on the table that are so bitter they're almost inedible. There's a plate that no-

body's allowed to eat off, and it has a bone on it, and a roasted egg. There's a full glass of wine that empties itself *without anyone touching it*. And some time during the seder, a piece of matza, the afikomen, disappears and I have never been able to find it.

MRS. HUDSON A piece of matza? You mean that crumbly cracker there?

REBECCA Yes. It looks just like that one. But I have to find it, Mr. Holmes, I just have to! Otherwise I won't grow up normally and my friends will stop speaking to me.

HOLMES Your message indicated that your brother has located the afikomen in the past. How do you account for this?

REBECCA I can't. Unless there's some sort of collusion between my brother and my father.

HOLMES And this book you enclosed, Miss Levy – what is its significance?

REBECCA That's the haggadah. It's in Hebrew. You're opening it from the wrong side.

HOLMES Oh, I beg your pardon.

REBECCA That's what everybody's reading at the seder when the wine and the afikomen disappear.

MRS. HUDSON *(scandalized)* Reading at the table?!

REBECCA Just once a year. Anyhow, we read it out loud.

HOLMES Would you tell us, briefly, what the haggadah contains?

REBECCA To tell you the truth, Mr. Holmes, it's pretty boring and I don't pay much attention. I can't remember much about it. Near the beginning, I ask the four questions, and my grandfather answers them; it takes a while. There's a song called *Dayenu*, and some vegetable-dipping and at the end the children go and open the door for Elijah and nobody's there.

HOLMES   This case presents some unusual aspects, Watson. Shall we have a closer look?

WATSON   I would be delighted if I can offer any assistance.

REBECCA   Thank you so much, Mr. Holmes! Would you like to come to our seder? It's tonight.

HOLMES   That will not be necessary, Miss Levy; if we can gain admittance to your home this afternoon, I think we may be able to clear up your little problem well before the festival begins.

REBECCA   I'll ask my mom.

MRS. HUDSON But, Mr. Holmes, you're expecting a visit from the King of Bavaria.

WATSON   In what connection?

HOLMES   Just a trifling matter of a royal sapphire and some incriminating letters. Certainly nothing on the scale of a crime that will echo through the ages, and place an entire civilization in peril.

WATSON   Great Scott, Holmes, whatever do you mean?

HOLMES   There's more trouble afoot than a mere missing cracker, Watson. I would not have missed this case for the world. Miss Levy, we shall await your wire. Mrs. Hudson, I perceive that you are about to visit the greengrocer. I would like to request that you bring back a specimen of *Armoracia rusticana.*

MRS. HUDSON Begging your pardon, Mr. Holmes?

HOLMES   A perennial plant related to the cabbage. When cut or grated, its root produces allyl isothiocyanate, which is a powerful irritant to the sinus and eyes. I believe I detect traces of this enzyme on Miss Levy's haggadah, and, having written a monograph on the varieties of mustard oil, I have some familiarity with its effects. I should like to test my theory.

MRS. HUDSON   And so what is it you're wanting, Mr. Holmes?

HOLMES   A horseradish.

MRS. HUDSON   Very good, sir.

WATSON   When the others had left, Holmes leaned back on the settee, closed his eyes and placed his finger-tips together, in a posture of a contemplation that I knew better than to interrupt. After some time, his eyes opened and he voiced his thoughts.

HOLMES   It is most peculiar. Here are the remnants of an ancient transgression. The bitterness of this odious root gives mute testimony to immense suffering; the matza is strong proof of haste and flight, almost certainly that of a people connected with the Levy family and their co-religionists. We are presented with evidence of an injustice on a massive scale. And yet young Miss Levy seems unaffected by the particulars, in spite of her having witnessed the presentation of that evidence annually.

WATSON   But, Holmes, how can you know that it's an *ancient* transgression? Surely this memory seems still fresh in the minds of the persecuted.

HOLMES   The imprint of the haggadah, Watson, reveals that it is in its eighty-second printing; and even so, it is tattered, worn and stained. One does not require an ability to read Semitic languages to see the indication of a very old story. And there has been no mention in the papers of a recent outrage against the Jews. I have never seen a case like it, Watson – the Levy family, along with millions of their tribe, have procured and safeguarded a wealth of clues for centuries, even millennia. And yet I cannot see either the nature of the crime, or any indication that the perpetrators have been brought to justice.

MRS. HUDSON   Mr. Holmes, a messenger has just come by asking you to call on Miss Levy at 130 Sidney Street at your earliest convenience.

HOLMES   Thank you, Mrs. Hudson. Well, Watson, we are off to Stepney. Do me the kindness of bringing your hat, and please discard that piece of toast you have stowed in your waistcoat pocket. It will not be welcome at the Levy home today.

WATSON   Holmes, I confess I am astounded that you knew I have a piece of toast.

HOLMES   There are fresh butter-stains all the way down to your watch-chain.

WATSON   We arrived in the East End amidst a flurry of activity. Pedlars of fish, fowl, linens, vegetables, and other assorted goods crowded the streets, pressed by matrons carrying bundles of varying sizes. The pace of commerce, and the cacaphony of voices, was overwhelming.

HOLMES   Ah, here we are. Note the small case nailed to the doorpost, Watson.

WATSON   What could that be?

HOLMES   A mezuza – an apotropaic device common in here in the East End. It indicates an ancient desire to turn away harmful influences, much like knocking on wood or placing gargoyles on a church. Why this particular device is nearly universally found on Jewish homes, is a story which may inform our investigation.

Just press the bell, Watson. I expect we shall soon

be able to connect these odd circumstances. Miss Levy, we are at your service.

REBECCA   Mr. Holmes, Dr. Watson! Thank you for your help.

WATSON   What an interesting aroma.

REBECCA   My mom just finished making gefilte fish.

WATSON   I beg your pardon – filtered fish?

HOLMES   'Gefilte,' Watson – German or Yiddish for 'filled.' The cook traditionally retains the whole skin of the fish, then stuffs it with spiced fish meal. Hence, 'filled fish.'

WATSON   Oh, I see.

HOLMES   Now, Miss Levy, if you would be kind enough to conduct us to the room where your seder is normally held.

REBECCA   Just over here, in the living room, Mr. Holmes. Most of the family sits in the lounge until the seder starts, and then we come in here.

HOLMES   I see the table is set for fifteen. Do the guests always sit in the same places from year to year?

REBECCA   Yes, now that my brothers and I are old enough to sit at the grownups' table. We used to have our own table.

HOLMES   This may be very important, Miss Levy. Can you remember, during the years when you sat at the children's table, whether the wine that magically emptied itself was at your table, or that of the adults?

REBECCA   I'm pretty sure it used to be on the children's table. Now it's on the big table.

HOLMES   And at what stage of the proceedings did that wine disappear?

REBECCA   While we were all looking for the afikomen – all the children, anyway.

HOLMES   Ah. Let me just have a look under this table *(pause)* and examine these chairs. I see the chairs are adorned with pillows – some sofa cushions, some bed pillows. Is this how you normally dine, Miss Levy?

REBECCA   No, Mr. Holmes, only at the seder. Papa says it's because we're free people. We can relax and eat. Not like slaves.

WATSON   Britons never, never, never shall be slaves, as the song goes.

REBECCA   But we *were* slaves. In the land of Egypt.

HOLMES   Indeed? When was that, Miss Levy?

REBECCA   A long time ago. It's in the Bible. I'm pretty sure that's why we have a seder.

HOLMES   So it says in your haggadah – at least, in the illustration on the cover, showing the affliction of slaves in the artistic style of ancient Egyptians. I wish I could penetrate the Aramaic text.

REBECCA   The haggadah's in Hebrew, Mr. Holmes.

HOLMES   If I may correct you, Miss Levy, the words look like Hebrew, and possibly even sound like Hebrew; but, according to the *Encyclopedia Britannica,* many of the haggadah's elements were composed at a time when Aramaic was the Jews' spoken language. Not quite Hebrew, although very close. Unfortunately, I am fluent in neither. Can you remember anything of the volume's contents, beyond what you've told us?

REBECCA   Well – a lot of it's the story of the Exodus – our ancestors leaving Egypt, that is. I know a lot about that.

WATSON   *Leaving* Egypt, you say; why did they do that?

REBECCA   Because they were slaves, of course! And they had horrible lives. So they had to escape, though Pharaoh wouldn't let them go.

HOLMES   Pray tell, what was it about their lives that was horrible?

REBECCA   They were forced to make bricks out of straw and mud, and build things for the Egyptians, and they had to work all day in the hot sun and they couldn't rest. And the taskmasters used to beat them, and even kill them if they wanted. And the Pharaoh told the Egyptians to throw all the baby boys in the Nile River to drown!

WATSON   You seem to have a very vivid recollection of these details, Miss Levy.

REBECCA   I should. They make us listen to it every year.

HOLMES   Observe the dinner table, Watson. There lies the horseradish, that repellent vegetable, representing the bitterness of slavery. And the bowls of – let me just confirm my hunch – yes, salt-water – bowls of *tears*, as it were, the tears of a weeping, oppressed people. These are placed here in accordance with no written instructions, Watson, but the strongest of traditions passed from Jewish parent to child for many centuries. And yet, how did this terrible injustice resolve? How came the Levy family, and all the others, to be celebrating in freedom? I feel the clue should be as apparent as the others, yet I cannot sense it.

REBECCA   Well, the slaves got out. They escaped. The Pharaoh was furious.

HOLMES	How did that come about?
REBECCA	It wasn't easy. Moses and Aaron asked permission at first, but that didn't work, so the Egyptians suffered ten plagues, starting with blood.
HOLMES	In what way was this a plague?
REBECCA	The water of the Nile River was turned into blood, until Moses turned it back.
HOLMES	And then?
REBECCA	Then frogs, lice, wild beasts, cattle disease, boils, hail, locusts, darkness, and finally the slaying of the firstborn.
WATSON	The firstborn? You mean, all the firstborn children?
REBECCA	No, just the firstborn children of the Egyptians.
HOLMES	That first plague was a warning, Watson. The Nile was turned to blood in plain sight of everyone, to advise the Egyptians that, if the Hebrews were not freed, it would all end in blood. Confronted with such a graphic caution, only the most incorrigible tyrant would fail to flinch.
WATSON	Hmm! Seems a reckless way to punish the Egyptians – casting about a deathly plague on the perpetrators without protecting the hostages.
REBECCA	But they *were* protected, Dr. Watson! The slaves were told to put the blood of the paschal sacrifice on their doorways, to protect them from the Angel of Death.
HOLMES	Blood and blood again, Watson. It appears to be an enduring theme. Especially, Miss Levy, as your family continues to protect itself the same way.
REBECCA	What do you mean, Mr. Holmes? We don't put blood on the doorway!

HOLMES	But you keep out the forces of evil the same way, with your mezuza. Guarding one's doors is an ancient and powerful instinct, not easily eroded by time. Whether consecrated blood or any other such item, it comes to the same thing.
REBECCA	Oh. Well, anyhow, the Pharaoh let the slaves go after that. But then he changed his mind, chased them through the Red Sea, and got drowned.
HOLMES	Fascinating. So the Hebrew civilization was saved, and entrusted with a mission to be witness forever to the hatefulness of oppression and the blessing of freedom. And here you are, Miss Levy, the latest generation charged with this duty.
REBECCA	I guess I am, if you put it that way. Sounds sort of important.
HOLMES	Indeed it is. Never more so, in this troubled world.
REBECCA	But, Mr. Holmes, what about the afikomen? How am I going to find it tonight?
HOLMES	Ah, I had almost forgotten. What, may I ask, is your father's occupation?
REBECCA	Why, he's a watchmaker.
HOLMES	I thought he might be, given the remarkable number of clocks in your home. And is he planning to train your brother in this profession?
REBECCA	As a matter of fact, he is. How did you know?
HOLMES	Miss Levy, have you ever wondered about this timepiece on the wall of your dining room? Have you noticed its unusual depth?
REBECCA	I can't say that I have.
HOLMES	I imagine you spend a good deal of time during your long seder looking at that clock, don't you?

REBECCA   I sure do.

HOLMES   And I feel confident that your brother does, too, but for a different reason. Do me the favor of opening the face of the clock. No, not the first door – there's a latch behind the clockworks. Open that.

REBECCA   It's an empty compartment!

HOLMES   Indeed it is, Miss Levy. I feel confident that, if you will allow your brother to open the door for Elijah this year, you will have enough time to retrieve the afikomen from behind the clock, and finally claim your prize. It's possible that you may also glimpse the draining of Elijah's wineglass by one of your more perceptible relatives.

REBECCA   Mr. Holmes! I can't thank you enough!

WATSON   You never fail to amaze me, Holmes. I'm sure I never would have found the afikomen. Especially after sitting through a big meal, feeling drowsy with that gefilte fish and all the rest passing through my – my – I can never remember the term for the canal of the digestive system.

HOLMES   It's alimentary, my dear Watson.

Matza Ball Soup

— a Marx Brothers play —

The Marx Brothers were the great anarchists of American comedy. No authority figure was safe from them, and no pretentious potentate could escape their wicked wit. The Marxes' antics were balm to battered American spirits coping with oppressive forces during the Great Depression and the Second World War.

And so in a book of interpretations of such a serious story – one of slavery and liberation, issues that are still current – I think the Marx Brothers have a proper place. Not only because the brothers themselves rehearsed the ritual every year in their Jewish home in New York's Upper East Side, but because it is a Jewish practice to bring down murderous dictators using ridicule. Just ask Mel Brooks. I think he would agree – and you can just chime in anytime, Mr. Brooks – that, had Jewish comedians been set loose in Ramses-era Egypt, one of the ten plagues would have been mockery. And that would have been a lot worse for Pharaoh than frogs.

In this *shpiel*, Groucho has the most lines. Zeppo and Margaret Dumont have the fewest lines, except for Harpo, who has no lines, but he honks. A bicycle horn would be useful for Harpo's portrayer.

MINNIE
SAM
GROUCHO
CHICO
HARPO
ZEPPO
MARGARET (DUMONT)

GROUCHO   Take a walk with me down memory lane, into the world of my childhood, full of love and laughter and the pungent aroma of boiled cabbage. Above a butcher shop on East 93rd Street in New York City – in that cozy homestead, my parents settled down to raise a family.

The twentieth century had only just begun, and it was a time of dreams and struggles. That's my mother, Minnie. To tell the truth, she's more Maxi. You can see her slaving over a hot stove. But you can't see the stove. She's the only Jewish mother on the Upper East Side who won't let her son become a doctor. She wants me to be a singer. I think she's been reading the script upside down.

And that's my father, Sam, the worst tailor in New York. He married my mother because he wanted children. Imagine his disappointment when *I* arrived.

You may know my brothers – Chico, Harpo, and Zeppo. With a little hard work they'll go a long way, and I wish they'd start now.

So, since you're here, I guess you'll be sharing our seder. It will be entirely your pleasure. Just don't ask too many questions. The seder's already long enough with this bunch of clowns running it. I don't know how I get through it myself, and if you think I'm stopping after four drinks you're crazy.

SAM	Minnie? I can't find the haggadahs. Where did we put them after the seder last year?
ZEPPO	Were they in a small brown cardboard box tied with bakery string, and marked 'mixed nuts'?
SAM	Yes!
ZEPPO	No, I haven't seen them.
CHICO	Hey, whatsamatter wit' these-a crackers, they taste just like-a the box they came in.
MINNIE	Chico, don't eat that matza, the seder's not even started yet. Where's Harpo? I told him he could assemble the seder plate.
ZEPPO	Last time I saw him, he was coming out of a pawn shop and heading for the race-track.
MINNIE	If he sold that seder plate again, he's going to be sorry. Harpo!
HARPO	*(honks)*
MINNIE	Have you put everything on the seder plate?
HARPO	*(honks)*
GROUCHO	He's roasting a goose egg.
MARGARET	Helloooo? Anyone home?
SAM	Oh, it's Mrs. Dumont. We're so glad you could come.
MARGARET	How kind of you, Mr. Marx. I'm delighted to be here. Everyone knows your seder is the social event of the season!
SAM	I wonder where she's getting *her* information? Boys, I'd like you to meet Mrs. Dumont.
GROUCHO	Pleased to meet you, Mrs. Dumont. I never forget a

face, but in your case I'll make an exception. Where's your husband?

MARGARET   Why, he passed away.

GROUCHO   I bet he's just using that as an excuse.

MINNIE   All right, everyone, it's time to get started. Let's sit down.

SAM   Groucho, since you're a bar mitsva now, would you like to start by saying the Kiddush?

GROUCHO   It will be a great honor. Especially if I get to drink the wine afterwards. Ah, here it is.

Baruh ata Adonai, elohaynoo meleh ha-olam, boray p'ree ha-gafen.

We praise You, Adonai our God, who together with the blessed sages of our people – the Manish-ewitz brothers, Baron Edmond de Rothschild, Johnny Walker Red, Jack Daniels, Jim Bean and Old Grand-Dad – created the fruit of the vine, and made us holy through Your commandments and that among these are life, liberty, and the pursuit of happiness, fraternité, égalité, Sleepy, Grumpy, Sneezy and Doc.

We praise You who have freed us from the bonds of sobriety, sustained us and brought us to this time, six sheets to the wind, off the wagon, feeling no pain, up a lazy river, with liberty and justice for all. And let us say: amen!

MARGARET   That was so moving, Groucho. I simply adore tra-dition!

SAM   Now, after everybody washes their hands …

GROUCHO   You can wash your neck, too, while you're at it.

SAM   … it's time to dip a vegetable in salt water.

CHICO	Make-a mine Scotch, I no like-a salt water so much.
SAM	*(Holds up matza.)* This is the bread of poverty, which our ancestors ate in the land of Egypt. It's time to ask the four questions. Boys?
ZEPPO	Why is this night different from all other nights? On other nights, we eat bread or matza; tonight, only matza.
CHICO	On all-a da other nights, we eat zucchini, peperone, pomodoro, spinaci – on this-a night, why we gotta eat this horsa-radish fra diavolo, it's so spicy it's-a gonna blow my head off.
GROUCHO	On all other nights we don't dip even once. Why, once I was dancing the cha-cha with Lulu Rosenthal and I tried to dip – it took a carthorse and a block and tackle two hours to get me off the floor. So on this night, why do we dip twice?
HARPO	*(Lies across two chairs and chews on a carrot.)*
ZEPPO	He wants to know why we eat while reclining.
MINNIE	Before we tell the story of the Exodus, someone should explain about the Four Sons.
GROUCHO	Mother, I thought you knew this already. When a man and a woman love each other very much …
SAM	That's enough out of you. There are four types of children, according to the rabbis. One who is wise, one who is wicked, one who is simple, and one who cannot even ask a question.
GROUCHO	We really have to get some new writers in here.
SAM	The wise son asks –
ZEPPO	What is the meaning of the decrees, laws, and rules that the Eternal has commanded us?

SAM	You should tell this child all the laws of Passover down to the last detail. The wicked son says –
GROUCHO	This is the silliest thing I *ever* heard.
SAM	To this child say: "This is done because of what the Eternal did for me when I went out of Egypt." The simple son asks –
CHICO	Whatsamatter you?
SAM	To this child, answer, "It was with a mighty hand that the Eternal brought us out of bondage." And to the child who cannot ask –
HARPO	*(honks)*
SAM	What's the point of saying anything to this child? He's just going to hang his leg over your arm.
HARPO	*(honks twice)*
MINNIE	Let's get on with the show, please. The brisket's going to burn.
GROUCHO	I wish to announce that a buffet supper will be served in the next room in five minutes. In order to get you in that room quickly, Mrs. Dumont will sing a soprano solo in *this* room.
SAM	Now it's time to tell the Passover story.
ZEPPO	A new king arose over Egypt who did not remember Joseph. And he said to his people:
CHICO	Look-a these Hebrew people here. Boy, we gotta lotta dese Hebrew people in Egypt. We gotta more Hebrew people in Egypt than they got pigeons in Central Park. Here's what we're-a gonna do: we're-a gonna oppress them with-a hard labor.
ZEPPO	You mean we're going to make them our slaves, mighty Pharaoh?

CHICO   That's-a what we're-a gonna do.

ZEPPO   Is this because you don't remember Joseph, great Pharaoh?

CHICO   Sure, I remember Giuseppe. We used-ta play-a stickball in the old neighborhood in Alexandria. Ah, Giuseppe – what a great stickball player! Now he's a-play minor league for the Cairo Cardinals.

ZEPPO   Mighty Pharaoh, I meant the Hebrew Joseph who saved Egypt from the famine and brought his family to live here. These are his descendants.

CHICO   No, I no remember-a Joseph.

SAM   But the more they oppressed them, the more numerous the Hebrews grew.

MINNIE   Then the Pharaoh told the Hebrew midwives to throw the Hebrew baby boys into the Nile River!

MARGARET   What an outrageous suggestion!

CHICO   It wasn't-a no suggestion!

SAM   To save her child, an Israelite woman from the tribe of Levi placed him in a basket lined with pitch, and put it among the reeds of the Nile. Sort of a little boat. Like a canoe.

GROUCHO   I wanted a flat bottom, but the girl at the boat house didn't have one.

SAM   The little boy's sister Miriam watched over him. The basket floated to where the Pharaoh's daughter was bathing in the Nile.

GROUCHO   She bathed once every four years. This accounts for the Nile's flooding. Also the extinction of the dinosaurs.

MARGARET   Why, it's an adorable little baby! I wonder if my father the Pharaoh will let me keep him. I shall name him Moses, for I drew him out of the water.

MINNIE   Oh, Princess! Would you like me to find a slave woman to care for the baby?

MARGARET   Why yes, little girl, I would be eternally grateful.

SAM   The lad grew up in the palace of the Pharaoh.

GROUCHO   One day I killed a taskmaster in my pajamas. How he got in my pajamas I'll never know. When word got out, I fled to the land of Midian and became a shepherd.

SAM   Baa!

GROUCHO   Why, hello, little fellow. You look like a sheep.

SAM   Baa!

GROUCHO   I think I've seen you before. Are you one of *my* sheep?

SAM   *(Slaps self on the forehead.)*

GROUCHO   I suppose you are. You all look alike to me. I think you're trying to get my attention.

SAM   I want you to look at that burning bush over there.

GROUCHO   Not much gets past you sheep, does it? I saw the burning bush. So what?

SAM   It's burning, but not being consumed.

GROUCHO   Really? *That* I didn't notice. I could be wrong but I think that's a miracle.

SAM   Moses, I think it wants to talk to you.

GROUCHO   Now I know where I've seen you before – it was in Bellevue.

MINNIE	Moses, Moses!
GROUCHO	Who are you?
MINNIE	I'm fine, who are you?
GROUCHO	I'm fine, too, but you can't come in unless you give the password.
MINNIE	Moses, I am the God of your ancestors. Remove your sandals, for the place where you stand is holy ground.
GROUCHO	Maybe I should go back to Bellevue. You sound an awful lot like my mother.
MINNIE	Such a son.
GROUCHO	So, God, what can I do for you?
MINNIE	Moses, I have seen the suffering of My people in Egypt, and have heard their cry. I have come to rescue them from slavery and bring them to a good and spacious land flowing with milk and honey.
GROUCHO	Make sure you wear a hat – the sun is brutal in Egypt this time of year.
MINNIE	*You* shall speak to Pharaoh and tell him to let My people go.
GROUCHO	*I* shall go to Pharaoh! So *that's* your game! Well, you can forget about that. I'm no rube. I'm going back into the closet where men are empty overcoats.
MINNIE	You shall plead with Pharaoh, but I shall harden Pharaoh's heart, and he will not let the people go.
GROUCHO	Now, why would you do a silly thing like that?
MINNIE	So that I may multiply My signs and wonders.
GROUCHO	Couldn't you do it faster with a calculator? Listen,

God, I can't speak to Pharaoh. First of all, I'm a wanted criminal, and second of all, I am slow of speech.

MINNIE   Slow of speech? Why, you never shut up!

GROUCHO   How could I possibly convince Pharaoh to give up hundreds of thousands of slaves?

MINNIE   I will be with you. And just because I like you, take along your brother Aaron to speak on your behalf.

GROUCHO   No kidding! Aaron? Why, I haven't seen him in years. So, he'll speak to Pharaoh, is that right?

HARPO   *(honks)*

GROUCHO   This is gonna be just great. I can hardly wait to go back to Egypt and see Pharaoh again. What great times we'll have – you, me, and that bicycle horn, in the dungeon, for the rest of our lives.

MINNIE   Aaron will create signs and wonders and Pharaoh will know that he faces a power greater than he.

SAM   And so Moses, with his brother Aaron by his side, returned to Egypt to free the Hebrew slaves.

GROUCHO   Okay, Aaron, you have everything you need to convince the Pharaoh to let our people go. These Egyptians are suckers for magic tricks. You've got a staff that turns into a snake, and a snake that turns into a staff. You've got a trick that turns your hand white. You've got a sea lion in your raincoat. You're a regular David Copperfield. According to a bush I met in Midian, the fix is in. Pharaoh will know a greater power than himself. What could possibly go wrong?

HARPO   *(honks)*

GROUCHO   Well, if Pharaoh's palace is in a hospital zone we might have a problem. Well, what do you know, here's the big mummy himself.

CHICO Hey, Moses! You look-a great! How long's it been?

GROUCHO Well, I'm eighty now, so it's been, what, eighty years?

CHICO You look-a fine. You married yet?

GROUCHO Yes, I was married not too long ago. I'll never forget my wedding day ... they threw vitamin pills.

CHICO So, Moses, what can-a I do fa you?

GROUCHO I'd like you to let the Hebrew slaves go, just long enough so they can have a seder in the wilderness. Then they'll be right back.

CHICO Ha! You no fool-a me! They're gonna go to the racetrack.

GROUCHO No, seriously, Pharaoh, you have to let my people go. If you don't, my ancestors would rise from their graves and I'd only have to bury them again.

CHICO The slaves, they-a stay right here.

GROUCHO Well, don't say I didn't warn you. Aaron, do your trick.

CHICO So he turn the stick into a snake. My magician, he can-a do that too. Hey, Zeppo!

ZEPPO Here goes! Wait, that wasn't supposed to happen.

GROUCHO Looks like your boy turned his staff into a duck. He forgot the magic word. Very impressive.

CHICO I spend thousands-a dollars to send him to magic school, and what do I get?

GROUCHO You get awfully tiresome after a while. Look, Pharaoh, since you're so hardhearted, I'm going to have to send a plague in your direction. The waters of the Nile have just turned to blood.

CHICO   Hey, turn it back! I can't stand da sight-a blood.

GROUCHO   Will you let the slaves go?

CHICO   Sure, why not?

ZEPPO   The Nile has just turned back to water again.

CHICO   Ots-a fine. Now, get outta here, I'm not lettin' da slaves go.

GROUCHO   I'd get really mad, but I know it's just the bush talking. Let's save some time here. Rather than go through all that again, what do you say I just tell you the next eight plagues? Frogs, lice, wild beasts, cattle disease, boils, hail, locusts, and darkness.

CHICO   I-a no let da slaves go because I gotta heartburn.

GROUCHO   I could sense that coming. What do you take for heartburn?

CHICO   Sometimes I take-a aspirin, an' sometimes I take-a calomel.

GROUCHO   I'd walk a mile for a – never mind, that's too easy. You know, I think you're the greatest Pharaoh that ever lived?

CHICO   Really?

GROUCHO   No, but I don't mind lying if it gets me somewhere … Pharaoh, you've been hit with nine plagues. All of them were highly unpleasant. Thus says the Lord, God of the Hebrews: so, what do you say, will you let the slaves go?

CHICO   Shut up you face and get outta here, Moses, we don't need no slaves no more in Egypt.

GROUCHO   Where shall I send the bill? That's six hundred thousand slaves, four hundred years each – even at a non-union rate, it's quite a pile of change, you must admit.

HARPO   *(honks)*

GROUCHO   Plus a delivery charge.

HARPO   *(honks twice)*

GROUCHO   Plus bricks and mortar.

CHICO   Ots-a fine. Take whatever you want.

GROUCHO   So, how does one get out of Egypt?

CHICO   Take-a left at Giza, cross the Nile Delta and then you get on-a da first cataract.

GROUCHO   That might be hard to see. Well, Pharaoh, it's been nice talking to you and I look forward to never seeing you again.

ZEPPO   Oh, great Pharaoh, how can you let the Hebrews go?

CHICO   *(whispering)* Don' worry, I gotta plan.

SAM   Before they left Egypt, Moses conveyed an interesting set of instructions to the Hebrews.

GROUCHO   I thought you were a sheep.

SAM   The sheep's part is over.

GROUCHO   I wouldn't bet on it.

SAM   Moses told the Hebrews to prepare for an unusual ritual before they left Egypt.

GROUCHO   Hebrews, may I have your attention, please. Every family is to take one lamb from the flock, and sacrifice it. Then put its blood all around your door.

ZEPPO   What a crackpot.

GROUCHO	In addition, you are instructed to avoid eating bread for a week, every year at this time.
MINNIE	Don't forget about the jewelry.
GROUCHO	Isn't that just like a woman! All right, then, everyone ask your neighbors to borrow their jewelry. If that works, ask to borrow all their shares of common stock. It's the least they owe us, considering all those years of hauling bricks, building pyramids, toting barges and lifting bales.
SAM	And at midnight, when the dreaded tenth plague struck Egypt, the children of Israel fled to the wilderness.
HARPO	*(honks)*
GROUCHO	Hey, what's the holdup? Where'd you learn to drive?
HARPO	*(honks)*
GROUCHO	Oh, now I see the problem. It's the sea. An enormous expanse of prime waterfront. Just when we thought we were free, we're stopped in our tracks. And I just put a security deposit on an apartment in Tel Aviv!
SAM	Suddenly, in the distance, Moses saw some strange figures.
GROUCHO	Exxon-Mobil 289, Apple 645, Alcoa 231 …
CHICO	You just wait till I catch up with you, I'm-a make you sorry you were ever born!
GROUCHO	It's the Pharaoh and his army! They're headed straight for us. This whole thing sphinx.
MINNIE	Moses! This is God again.
GROUCHO	You better talk fast.

MINNIE	Moses, hold your staff over the waters, and they will part.
GROUCHO	At this point I'll try anything.
SAM	And Moses parted the waters of the Red Sea, and the Israelites walked through to the other side.
HARPO	*(honks)*
GROUCHO	The Egyptians are walking through the Red Sea, too. Ain't that a kick in the pants.
MINNIE	Just wait.
CHICO	Hey, Moses, come back here! You an-a me gonna settle this once and-a for all!
GROUCHO	Now, let's be reasonable about this.
CHICO	Are you a man or a mouse?
GROUCHO	Put a piece of cheese on the ground and you'll find out.
SAM	As the Egyptians followed the Hebrews through the Red Sea, suddenly the waters closed again and the Egyptian army was drowned.
ZEPPO	Why didn't I bring my swimmies?
GROUCHO	I got Pharaoh a good steady position in a pyramid. Horizontal! Let it never be said that I don't take care of my friends.
SAM	Boys, you've done a fine job, and you've been very patient sitting through the seder. But it's not over. There's someone outside who wants to come in.
GROUCHO	If it's my bookie, you haven't seen me all day!
SAM	No, it's Elijah, the invisible guest who visits every seder in the world. Chico, why don't you go and open the door for him?

CHICO   I don't think so. He's-a come in and drink up all-a da wine!

MARGARET   But it would be a great honor to meet such a distinguished visitor! Mrs. Marx, I appeal to you, please admit Mr. Elijah.

CHICO   No, first I think I'm-a gonna sing "Dayenu."

GROUCHO   Go sing next to that window and I'll help you out.

CHICO   *If I had some tootsi-frootsi,*
             You can bet you sweet pitootsie,
             Tootsi-frootsi, sweet pitootsie, Dayenu!

ZEPPO   Everybody! Day-dayenu, day-dayenu, day-dayenu – dayenu, dayenu!

GROUCHO   There's my argument. Restrict immigration.

MINNIE   Groucho, do as your father tells you and go open the door for Elijah.

GROUCHO   I guess there's no getting out of this one. All right, I'm opening the door. Elijah, you sly dog – you want to come in?

CHICO   Depends. What's the password? I give you three guesses.

GROUCHO   Let's see – is it horseradish?

CHICO   No, it's-a no horseradish.

GROUCHO   Is it haroset?

CHICO   No. Hey, I tell you what – it's a kind of fish.

GROUCHO   A kind of a fish? Is it herring?

CHICO   No.

GROUCHO   Is it a mackerel?

CHICO	No. What's-a da thing you put the coffee grounds in?
GROUCHO	The filter?
CHICO	That's-a right, you got it! Da-filter fish.
GROUCHO	All right, Elijah, I guess you can come in.
CHICO	Hey, a glassa wine! Here's mud in your eye!
MARGARET	Where did he go? He was just here!
MINNIE	He never stays long – he has a lot of Manishevitz to put away tonight.
SAM	All right, that about wraps it up for the seder …
ZEPPO	Wait a minute, you can't stop here!
GROUCHO	A seder should begin at the beginning and end at the ending. Anything less isn't right. Those are my principles, and if you don't like them, well, I've got others. What about our favorite songs? Like the one little goat that my father bought for two zuzim plus stock options?
HARPO	*(honks)*
GROUCHO	That's right, what about the afikomen? You don't think you're getting away with *that*, do you? A fine father *you* turned out to be! Taking dry crackers from your family's mouths! Chico, go find that afikomen!
CHICO	Eh, you want I should-a steal?
ZEPPO	Oh, no, no! It's not stealing.
CHICO	Well, then, I couldn't do it.
ZEPPO	But we *have* to find it!
CHICO	Harpo, he can-a find it. Why, he got a nose just

like-a bloodhound.   And the rest-a his face don't look so good either.

SAM   Harpo, get your hand out of my pocket!

MINNIE   Very good, son, you've found the afikomen.

CHICO   You want-a da afikomen, we give you a good deal. One dollar.

GROUCHO   One dollar?

CHICO   One dollar and you'll remember me all your life.

GROUCHO   That's the most nauseating proposition I've ever had.   All right, fine.   Father, we'd like to present you with this afikomen.   You'll need it to finish this seder.   I have nothing but confidence in you, and very little of that.

SAM   We conclude the seder with these inspiring words: next year in Jerusalem!

GROUCHO   I'd settle for Palm Springs.

MARGARET   My dear Mr. and Mrs. Marx, thank you so much for your kind invitation.

GROUCHO   Mrs. Dumont, I've had a perfectly wonderful evening, but unfortunately this wasn't it.

My friends, that's it for the seder, the most fun you can have in a small room with two dozen relatives. It's nice to see you, but I've got nobody to blame but myself.   You're welcome to come back tomorrow for our second seder; just follow the trail of matza crumbs up Lexington Avenue.   For now, I think I've earned a nice after-dinner cigar.   Ta-ta!

Harry Potter and the Deathly Horseradish

Ever since *Harry Potter and the Sorcerer's Stone,* I have had my suspicions about Hermione. She has an academic bent, and she shares a first name with the late Hermione Gingold, the British Jewish actress. And as Hermione points out herself in this shpiel, "Both my parents are dentists and I spend my spare time organizing elf labor unions." Great Britain is home to 300,000 Jews, and I simply think Hermione is one of them.

Much has been made of the major conflict in the Potter books, which pits an idealistic group of wizards and witches against an evil warlord aiming at world domination. Lord Voldemort, who gathers his followers using a combination of threats and promises of glory, is especially incensed by racial impurity among wizards; those who are descended from regular humans are 'mudbloods' and must be eliminated. Hermione herself is a mudblood and a special target of Voldemort. The Nazi analogy is unquestionable.

The strongest element of Jewish philosophy in the series is articulated in a conversation between Harry and his very rabbinical-looking headmaster, Albus Dumbledore, near the end of *Chamber of Secrets.* "It is our choices, Harry, that show what we truly are, far more than our abilities." This affirms that, more than belief, we are defined by our freely-chosen actions. It's a rejection of concepts foreign to Judaism, such as original sin and predestination. Our Jewish obligation is to work towards the world's repair. To choose this path is not only to reveal our character, but also to become closer to the Divine.

Our civilization was the first to separate religion from magic. Attempting to influence nature using language, ritual, or symbol, was forbidden – such interference was strictly God's function, in biblical times. However, the manipulation of natural phenomenon certainly is illustrated in the ten plagues against Egypt, and the other 'signs and wonders' performed by Moses and Aaron. Jewish mystics still do try to guide human fortunes by these means. So magic has its place in our lore, if not our philosophy, and who better to explain the magic of the Exodus and the sym-

49

bols of the seder than our very own Hermione?

This lengthy shpiel has a large number of roles. The major ones are Hermione, Harry, Ron, and Dumbledore. If needed, roles that could be combined in one actor might be Hagrid and Hannah Abbott, Luna and Fred, and George and Draco. Possibly also Ron and Snape, and Dumbledore and McGonagall.

Charms, jinxes, hexes and spells which are not explained in the text, are footnoted.

HARRY
HERMIONE
RON
(PROFESSOR) DUMBLEDORE
DRACO
(PROFESSOR) SNAPE
(PROFESSOR) McGONAGALL
HAGRID
FRED (WEASLEY)
GEORGE (WEASLEY)
LUNA (LOVEGOOD)
HANNAH (ABBOTT)

RON	This is the absolute best class at Hogwarts! A seminar! We only have homework one week a term. The rest of the sessions we just sit around watching the other students sweat in the spotlight.
GEORGE	And anybody can sign up for Comparative Magic. Every week we get to see you cute little under-classmen pretending to be grownups.
DRACO	And *this* week we can catch up on sleep – it's Granger's turn to do her presentation.
RON	Watch it, Malfoy!
HARRY	I don't know why you're sounding so smug, Mal-foy. Hermione's sure to get high honors in Com-parative Magic, and you'll be lucky to pass.
DRACO	I repeat my earlier statement. This session will be a snoozer. I don't know why she had to schedule this at night.
RON	Draco, I'm warning you, if you do anything to in-terfere with Hermione's presentation – bloody hell, what's she carrying?
HERMIONE	Hello, everyone! Harry and Ron, would you please

pass these out?

FRED   Why on earth have you brought an encyclopedia, Hermione?

HERMIONE   This is *not* an encyclopedia, Fred. It's a set of *haggadot*. Everyone gets one.

GEORGE   Leave it to Hermione to give us a reading assignment.

HERMIONE   We'll all be reading it together, George. Don't worry, it's easy – I've read it every spring since I was little.

DRACO   Is that some sort of Muggle custom?

HERMIONE   Yes, it's a sort of Jewish Muggle custom.

RON   Hermione, I didn't know you were Jewish!

HERMIONE   Honestly, Ron! Both my parents are dentists and I spend my spare time organizing elf labor unions. What *else* would I be?

MᶜGONAGALL Good evening, my dear students. I am very much looking forward to tonight's festivities. Miss Granger, I've brought the candles and goblets you requested.

FRED   Festivities?

FEORGE   Goblets?

FRED   This sounds like fun.

GEORGE   I'll take charge of the fireworks.

MᶜGONAGALL Mr. Weasley, there are no fireworks allowed during the Comparative Magic seminar. This week's presenter will explain the procedures. Miss Granger, you have our complete attention.

HERMIONE   Thank you, Professor, and thank you for bringing the supplies.   Now then, before anything begins, we are all to wash our hands. Pitchers, bowls and towels have just appeared in front of each of you.

We are about to re-enact the tradition known as the 'seder.' It is practiced by both Muggle and magical communities, and it commemorates an ancient sequence of events that is sacred to the Jews. In essence, the Hebrews in Egypt were enslaved by –

DRACO   *(snores)*

HERMIONE   – were enslaved by the *evil Pharaoh,* and their liberation was accomplished through pioneering spells cast by Moses and his brother Aaron, the Hebrews' chief magician. This memory is essential to the formation of the Jewish people.

DUMBLEDORE I beg pardon for my late arrival. May I join the session, Miss Granger? I would very much like to witness this interesting ritual.

HERMIONE   Of course, Headmaster, I'm so glad you're here. Tonight, as you are all aware, is the full moon after the northern vernal equinox –

DUMBLEDORE Which is why Professor Lupin sends his regrets.

HERMIONE   I completely understand. To continue, before the seder ceremony, all items containing leavening are to be removed from the premises. Although in the Muggle world, this is only achieved through days of hard work, we simply use an obliteration charm. *(Picking up and waving wand.)* It's a fairly simple spell: *Expello hametzum!*[1]

FRED   Hey! Bring back my cauldron cake!

HERMIONE   No cauldron cakes at the seder, Fred. Also, no bread, spaghetti, biscuits or breakfast cereal. So, we light these candles in honor of the festival. To abbreviate, we won't recite the *Benedictus es Adonai,* and just use the *incendio* spell.[2]

FRED   Bzzzzt! Bzzzzt!

HERMIONE   They're just basic wax candles, George, not Ever-
              lasting Sparklers. In the course of the ritual, each
              participant will drink four cups of the fruit of the
              vine. I suppose it's all right if we use pumpkin
              juice. Professor McGonagall has kindly provided
              self-refilling goblets, so we won't have to waste
              time pouring.

              Next we present the unleavened bread, the bread of
              poverty, which is called 'matza' in Hebrew. This is
              accompanied by an incantation in Aramaic which
              invites all who are hungry to come and eat: *kal
              dikhfeen yaytay v'yaykhol*. And the matza is broken
              in two pieces, and the larger piece is wrapped in
              something like a small invisibility cloak.

RON   Will we need it again? How are we going to find
              it?

HERMIONE   It's not an *actual* invisibility cloak, it's just a napkin
              with a disillusionment charm on it. And, yes, we
              will need it again, because we can't conclude the
              seder without it. So someone's going to have to
              protect it.

GEORGE   Here, I'll do it. I'll just put a Protego hex[3] on it.
              Clamatis azymos![4]

RON   (*shrieks*)

McGONAGALL   Mr. Weasley, that was a Screeching charm, and you
              missed the matza. Why don't I just keep it next to
              me, under the Sorting Hat. It's safe enough there.

HERMIONE   We'll proceed with the explanation of the four chil-
              dren. The haggadah instructs us to teach everyone
              the story, regardless of that person's ability to –

DRACO   What a bore!

HERMIONE — that person's *ability to understand*, or their *attitude*. So everyone will become part of the story. There's the wise child, the wicked child, the simple child, and the child who doesn't know how to ask. A Ravenclaw student will represent the wise child, Slytherin the wicked child, Hufflepuff the simple child, and Gryffindor the child who cannot ask.

DUMBLEDORE Well done, my child.

HERMIONE Thank you. Ravenclaw, please read aloud from the middle of page 347.

LUNA The wise child asks, "What is the meaning of the charms, jinxes, curses and hexes that have been set before us?" You should give this child the Standard Book of Spells, grades one through seven, by Miranda Goshawk, plus supplementary readings.

HERMIONE Slytherin, please continue.

DRACO The wicked child asks, "Why are we bothering with this endless chattering when there's a fantastic feast hovering overhead, waiting to be eaten?" To this child you should say, "This ritual is for us who have chosen to be included in the community. One who excludes himself will have his dinner enchanted by a Banishing charm."

HERMIONE Now it's Hufflepuff's turn.

HANNAH The simple child asks: "What is this?" To this child you should say, "It was with a mighty arm and a phoenix-feather wand that the Almighty brought us out of Egyptian bondage."

HERMIONE Finally, Gryffindor.

HARRY/RON/FRED/GEORGE To the child who doesn't know enough to ask, you should begin as it is written: "It is because of what the great sorcerers of ancient times did for me when I went free from Egypt."

HERMIONE   Now, traditionally, the youngest person at the se-
            der asks the four questions, which introduces the
            story of the exodus from slavery. I'm not sure who
            the youngest person present is; Harry, are you the
            youngest here?

HARRY   I suppose I am. What four questions?

HERMIONE   Right there at the top of 361.

HARRY   That's not in English, Hermione.

HERMIONE   I find it's easier to use a translation charm. *Trans-
            forma anglicorem!*[5]

HARRY   All right then. Why is this night different from all
            other nights? On other nights we eat any kind of
            bread that appears before us; on this night, only
            matza. On other nights, we eat any vegetable that
            Professor Sprout says is in season; on this night,
            only bitter herb. On other nights, we don't dip our
            dinner in a Pensieve at all; tonight, we dip twice.
            On other nights, we eat while sitting normally in a
            chair, or hovering several inches above the floor; on
            this night, only hovering.

HERMIONE   That's lovely. Now, everyone take a stalk of pars-
            ley and dip it in the salt water. Like this. Ugh!
            What's happened to the salt water?

GEORGE   My goodness, Hermione, it seems to have turned
            into marshmallow fluff.

McGONAGALL Mr. Weasley, you can hand me your wand right
            now.

HERMIONE   Well, moving along, we recall the bitterness of
            slavery by eating the bitter herb. This is the most
            resentful, harshest of vegetables, the mandrake.
            Everyone should take a bite of it.

RON   Ow! It bit back!

MᶜGONAGALL   Perhaps they're not quite ripe yet.

HERMIONE   Well, now we know the bitterness of slavery. Let's proceed with the telling of the Exodus story. It's much more interesting if we each take a role and re-enact the events. I'll begin with a bit of narration.

A new Pharaoh arose over Egypt who didn't remember Joseph. He saw that the Hebrews were very numerous, and he said …

SNAPE   May I ask why all these students are occupying the Great Hall at night?

MᶜGONAGALL   Professor Snape! We weren't expecting you.

DUMBLEDORE   My dear Professor, I hope you'll join us. I think there's definitely a place for you here. Would you honor us by reading some passages from this book?

SNAPE   Very well. Let us put taskmasters over them, and afflict them with hard labor.

HERMIONE   But the more he afflicted them, the more they increased. So he said …

SNAPE   Let all the baby boys of the Hebrews be thrown into the Nile to drown, but the girls you shall let live.

HERMIONE   But the midwives would not, and they explained to the Pharaoh …

MᶜGONAGALL   The Hebrew women are lively, and by the time we arrive, they have already given birth and hidden the children. That's really all Pharaoh needs to know.

HERMIONE   One woman of the Levite tribe gave birth to a baby boy. She made a basket and lined it with pitch; putting the baby into it, she floated it down the Nile River. Harry?

HARRY   The baby was guarded by his sister Miriam, who
             followed it downstream until it was discovered by
             the daughter of the Pharaoh.

HANNAH   It is most probably a Hebrew child. I will name
             him Moses, for I drew him out of the water.

HARRY   And the Pharaoh's daughter raised the baby as her
             own. Hermione, was she nice to him? Or did she
             make him sleep under the staircase?

HERMIONE   Harry, it was Pharaoh's palace. Even the rooms
             under the staircases were awesome.

HARRY   All right. When Moses grew up, he saw a taskmas-
             ter beating a slave.

DRACO   Take that, you low-born disgusting Hebrew! If you
             don't work faster I'll crack your skull!

DUMBLEDORE   It's a difficult action to take, but under the circum-
             stances, one must save an innocent life. *Avada Ke-
             davra!*[6]

HARRY   Moses struck the taskmaster down, and hid his
             body in the sand.   But Moses' action was wit-
             nessed. The next day, seeing two Hebrew slaves
             fighting with each other, Moses tried to break it up.
             And the slaves said to him:

FRED/GEORGE Are you going to kill us as you did the Egyptian?

DUMBLEDORE   Much to my regret, I must flee Egypt to the safety
             of Midian. Is one of the hippogryffs available?

HERMIONE   Alone in the wilderness, Moses had a strange en-
             counter: he witnessed a bush that was burning, but
             was not consumed.

DUMBLEDORE   What a remarkable sight. Is this some ancient spell,
             or merely a new variety of floo powder? I must get
             closer and see.

LUNA	Moses! I have heard the cries of My people en-slaved in Egypt. You will go to Pharaoh with signs and wonders, and he will let My people go.
DUMBLEDORE	*I* shall go? But I am slow of speech. Pharaoh will not listen to me.
LUNA	Don't be afraid, Moses. I will send your brother Aaron with you, and he will speak. Pharaoh will yet face a power mightier than his own.
HARRY	Moses, I have been given a wand that turns into a serpent. All I have to do is speak to it in Parsel-tongue. And I can make your hand turn white as snow, and then turn it back to normal. Plus I have a wicked bunch of plagues that Sirius Black gave me. Let's go!
HERMIONE	Aaron, you see, was a Secret-Keeper, so his pres-ence was necessary in the visit to Pharaoh. And Moses and Aaron came before Pharaoh, to ask him to let the Hebrews go free.
DUMBLEDORE	Pharaoh, I ask you to let my people go.
SNAPE	You'll soon learn that your fame doesn't get you everything you want. I will not let the slaves go.
HERMIONE	After several preliminary demonstrations, Moses told Aaron to hold his wand over the Nile River, and that turned the waters of Egypt to blood.
LUNA	Was it really blood, or did they use a Color-Changing Charm?
HERMIONE	The story doesn't say. Anyway, Pharaoh remained unimpressed.
SNAPE	No, no, no! I will not let them go!
HERMIONE	Then Moses warned the Pharaoh:
DUMBLEDORE	Pharaoh, I must inform you that if you do not free

the slaves, something very unpleasant will creep out of the Nile.

HARRY *Accio ranae!*[7]

RON Chocolate frogs! I don't think this is unpleasant at all! Thanks, Hermione! *(pause)* Ugh! Disgusting!

McGONAGALL Mr. Weasley, take this opportunity to learn that things are not always what they seem.

HAGRID Them's Nile frogs, Ron. They're as brown as fudge. Here, drink some of this, as'll wash out the taste a bit.

HERMIONE Thank you, Hagrid. I didn't notice you over there.

HAGRID I heard there was goin' teh be beasts.

HERMIONE There will be. Now, the Pharaoh relented when he saw the frogs all over Egypt, but when they were gone, he once again became hardhearted. It's possible that he was under an Imperio curse.[8]

DUMBLEDORE Harry – that is, Aaron – use your wand to strike the dust of the earth.

DRACO And all the dust turned to lice throughout the land of Egypt. Pharaoh, this is the finger of God!

SNAPE Be still!

HERMIONE Three terrible plagues still had not moved Pharaoh. Moses and Aaron cast a Protego Totalum charm[9] over Goshen, where the Hebrews lived; and because of that, no insects touched any Hebrew slave.

HANNAH Hermione, I'm sorry for interrupting, but I think there's a dragon under the table.

DRACO What's that in the punch bowl – looks like a sea serpent.

LUNA Pixies! How cute.

HERMIONE   The next plague to strike Egypt was that of wild
                  beasts. Uh, Hagrid ... could you ... possibly con-
                  trol that dragon?

HAGRID   'E won't hurt anybody – here, Tulip! Come 'ere,
                  boy! Now, don't – um, I need a bucket o' water.

MᶜGONAGALL   *Accio aquae.*[10]   Hagrid, please douse that fire and
                  put the dragon outside. Miss Granger, have the
                  wild beasts sufficiently demonstrated this plague?

HERMIONE   Yes, of course, I'm sorry, Professor McGonagall.
                  The wild beasts, or some say swarms of flies, over-
                  ran Egypt until Pharaoh asked Moses to remove
                  them and promised to free the Hebrews. But once
                  they were gone –

SNAPE   I refuse to let the slaves go. I am, after all, the
                  mighty Pharaoh.

HERMIONE   The next plague gave me a bit of a problem.

HARRY   It's Hedwig! Hedwig, what's wrong? She looks
                  flushed. She has a fever!

RON   There's Filch's cat – she looks worse than Hedwig.

HERMIONE   I'm sorry, but I couldn't find a spell to create cattle
                  disease.

DUMBLEDORE   So you improvised. Cat and owl disease. Bravo,
                  Miss Granger.

MᶜGONAGALL   Hannah, please administer a healing charm for
                  those creatures.

HERMIONE   The plague killed the Egyptians' livestock, but left
                  the Hebrews' animals unharmed. Next, Aaron cast
                  a Furnunculus curse[11] on the Egyptians, causing
                  them to be covered with boils, even the wizards.
                  Once again, the Hebrews were unaffected.

LUNA   Why hasn't the Pharaoh given up yet? It's obvious he's going to lose.

HERMIONE   Because he's unable to. His heart was controlled by an unseen force.

LUNA   Perhaps all these demonstrations of power weren't to teach *him*, but to teach the Hebrews.

DUMBLEDORE   In the interest of time, we should return to the text. Next comes a Meteolojinx,[12] producing a great hailstorm on the land of the Egyptians.

HARRY   The Pharaoh was unnerved, but only temporarily. As soon as Moses and Aaron stopped the hail, he again decided he would not let the Israelites go.

DUMBLEDORE   Pharaoh, I must warn you that the next plague will be a swarm of locusts that will consume all the grain of your people. They will cover the surface of Egypt, and they will fill your palaces and your houses.

HERMIONE   The locusts consumed everything; not a tree or a plant remained.

GEORGE   Look! The mandrakes ran under the Sorting Hat.

SNAPE   Very well, since you persist, I will permit the Hebrew men to leave, but the women, children and property shall remain.

HERMIONE   That wasn't acceptable. The ninth plague was a Nox charm[13], on a scale that has never been duplicated. Darkness covered all of Egypt for three days – except for the homes of the Hebrews.

LUNA   My goodness, I can't even see my own hand in front of my face.

RON   I'm trying for a Lumos charm[14], but my wand isn't working!

FRED   That's your butter-knife.

SNAPE	Enough! All the Hebrews may leave. But their property stays behind.

| DUMBLEDORE | Pharaoh shall soon encounter a power beyond his own. At midnight tonight, the first-born of everyone in Egypt shall be slain – from Pharaoh atop his throne, to the flobberworm at the bottom of the river. But not a bowtruckle shall even snarl at any of the Israelites. Then Pharaoh and his court shall bow to me and beg the Israelites to depart. |

| SNAPE | Highly doubtful. |

| HERMIONE | Then Moses and Aaron were given instructions to pass on to the enslaved Hebrews. |

| HARRY | Every family must take a lamb from its flock, and sacrifice it at twilight. Put some of its blood on the two doorposts of your houses. This will act as a Cave Inimicum, a spell that strengthens an enclosure against enemies. At midnight, every Egyptian home will be visited by a Dementor, which will steal the soul of the firstborn. |

| DRACO | I wouldn't wish that on anybody. |

| DUMBLEDORE | No? You surprise me, Mr. Malfoy. All's fair in love and war. |

| LUNA | And the Hebrews were fighting for their lives. |

| HANNAH | I didn't realize there were Dementors back then. |

| HERMIONE | I read that they were a metaphor for clinical depression. Anyway, the Hebrews performed this ritual and escaped from Egypt. But it was not long before … |

| SNAPE | What have we done? Send chariots after the slaves! Bring them back! |

| HARRY | And the Egyptians gave chase, and overtook the Hebrews by the shore of the Red Sea. |

GEORGE   The Hebrews cried out to Moses: weren't there enough graves in Egypt, that you've taken us out here to die in the wilderness? What have you done to us?

DUMBLEDORE   Moses answered: have no fear, for the Egyptians you see before you, you shall never see again.

FRED   And Moses lifted his wand and held it over the sea, and split it, so that the Hebrews were able to walk through it on dry land.

RON   That's incredible.

MᶜGONAGALL   Unfortunately, nearly all the geography spells have been lost. The splitting of the sea has occurred only once in recorded history. There have been many attempts at sea-splitting, usually just after earthquakes, but none were successful.

DRACO   Didn't really solve the problem, though, did it? If the Hebrews could walk through, so could the Egyptians.

DUMBLEDORE   The Egyptians, their horses and chariots, came in pursuit after them into the sea, but at Moses' command, the waters turned back and covered them.

LUNA   The Israelites were safe, and Miriam the prophet led them in song and dance!

HANNAH   Hermione, is that the end of the story?

HERMIONE   Not the end, really – the former slaves went into the wilderness, where they had a massive encounter at a mountain called Sinai. But that's not really part of the story told at the seder.

SNAPE   Since you seem to have no further role for me, I take my leave. Fifth-form students, recall that you have a major examination in the morning.

RON   Leave it to Snape to spoil a perfectly lovely evening.

DUMBLEDORE   This has been a fascinating – I suppose you would call it a story?

HERMIONE   When it's told during the seder, the story of the Exodus is called the 'maggeed,' the telling.

DUMBLEDORE   Ah. And what happens after the maggeed, Miss Granger?

HERMIONE   After another handwashing, everyone tastes the matza, the bread of poverty, and the bitter herb combined with the sweetness of haroset, which is a nuts-and-apples potion. And then we eat a huge meal …

GEORGE   Brilliant!

M^cGONAGALL   The huge meal will be postponed till after class.

FRED   That's a rotten shame.

HERMIONE   And everyone drinks four glasses of wine.

FRED   Now you're talking!

M^cGONAGALL   And the four glasses of wine will be postponed until you're of legal age.

HERMIONE   Then there's a great deal of spoken ritual that reflects the celebration of freedom; and we open the door to admit Elijah.

DRACO   Does he always arrive late? What a rude person.

HERMIONE   Elijah is permitted to come to the seder any time he likes, given that he's over 2,800 years old and has to visit every seder on earth.

DUMBLEDORE   Clearly he possessed the Philosopher's Stone long before Nicolas Flamel. I shouldn't like to have the burden of his schedule, though. What occupies Elijah for the rest of the year, Miss Granger?

HERMIONE   Oh, he's pretty busy all the time, Headmaster. He visits the deserving poor disguised as a beggar, and he also attends the covenant ceremony of every newborn Jewish baby.

DUMBLEDORE   Great Merlin's beard!

McGONAGALL   Then perhaps we shouldn't keep him waiting.

HERMIONE   Ron, would you please go open the door?

RON   Sure.

(Crashing sound.)

DUMBLEDORE   Peeves, you are banished from the premises until the end of term. Elijah, if you are here among us, we offer our respectful greetings, and a large goblet of pumpkin juice.

HERMIONE   The seder concludes with everyone sharing the afikomen, the matza that was set aside at the beginning of the seder. Does anyone know where it is?

HARRY   Professor McGonagall put it under the Sorting Hat.

GEORGE   Well, there's nothing under it now.

LUNA   That's curious. Did Hagrid take it away with the dragon?

RON   I don't think he did. What about the mandrakes? They were in the Sorting Hat too.

HANNAH   They ran back to the herbarium. Didn't you hear them shrieking?

McGONAGALL   Mr. Weasley – George Weasley – would you please go ask Professor Sprout to question the mandrakes.

DRACO   Don't know what the mandrakes could want with matza.

HERMIONE   Just a moment. Professor McGonagall, did you say you put the afikomen under the Sorting Hat?

MᶜGONAGALL   Yes, I did put it there.

HERMIONE   Well, what usually happens to things under the Sorting Hat?

HARRY   *(pause)* They get sorted!

HERMIONE   Exactly! To where?

HARRY   To the place where they truly belong. So where would the Sorting Hat send the afikomen?

DRACO   Something that dry and dull must have been sent to the Weasleys!

RON   No, it went to *your* house, Malfoy. It's tasteless, remember?

DUMBLEDORE   The Sorting Hat divines the essence of its subject; Miss Granger, what is the afikomen's essence?

HERMIONE   It's the last thing we eat at the meal. It's baked quickly, without any yeast, and it doesn't rise like bread, because it symbolizes humility.

DUMBLEDORE   What did you tell us, when you first showed us the afikomen?

HERMIONE   I said, this is the bread of poverty, which we eat on the festival of freedom to remember slavery. All who are hungry, let them come and eat.

HARRY   The afikomen is about humility and liberation. I think I know where it is.

RON   Harry, where are you going?

HARRY   I'll be right back.

GEORGE   The afikomen isn't in the herbarium. By the way, Harry almost knocked me over in the doorway.

FRED   He thinks he knows where it is.

McGONAGALL   Miss Granger, while we wait for the afikomen's return, I wish to tell you that this was an excellent presentation of Comparative Magic. I am awarding a hundred points to Gryffindor, and you'll be receiving a First in this subject.

DRACO   No fair! I didn't get any points for Slytherin when I did *my* presentation!

McGONAGALL   Mr. Malfoy, your card trick was not sufficient illumination of the study of Comparative Magic. Tonight, I believe, we all learned something.

HARRY   Here's the afikomen!

RON   Brilliant!

HERMIONE   Harry, you've saved the seder.

DRACO   It's just a cracker, it's not a Golden Snitch!

DUMBLEDORE   Tell us, Harry, where did you find it?

HARRY   The Sorting Hat sent the afikomen to Dobby. He's very humble, and he's been personally redeemed from slavery. When I went to see him, he was waving an invisible napkin and shouting, "Dobby is a free elf!"

DUMBLEDORE   Dobby is truly the spirit of the seder. One little elf, who was purchased for less than two zuzim.

McGONAGALL   Well done, Harry. Students, help yourselves to the feast and then make sure you clean up all the matza crumbs. I want to see those brooms flying!

[1] I just made this up.

[2] The *Incendio* charm produces fire, and was used, for example, by Hagrid in *Sorcerer's Stone.*

[3] The *Protego* is a shield charm, preventing jinxes, curses and hexes from having their full effect.

[4] *Clamatis azymos* is a form of the Caterwauling Charm.

[5] I made this one up, too.

[6] The *Avada Kedavra* curse inflicts immediate, painless death upon its target. Its name is derived from the Aramaic 'abracadabra,' which means 'I shall create according to the word.'

[7] This *accio* or summoning charm conjures frogs.

[8] The *Imperio* curse causes its target to obey the commands of the caster.

[9] This shield charm would protect its target from all malevolent forces.

[10] This charm summons water.

[11] The *Furnunculus* curse, which covers the target in boils, is found in *Goblet of Fire* where it hit Goyle instead of Harry's intended target, Draco.

[12] The *Meteolojinx* produces weather effects.

[13] The Nox charm, found in *Prisoner of Azkaban* and *Deathly Hallows,* darkens the surrounding area.

[14] The *Lumos* charm produces light from the end of a wand.

Much Ado About Bupkes

— a Shakespeare play —

It is extremely unlikely that Shakespeare ever met a Jew, although tantalizing theories have been floated about a possible collaborator of *The Merchant of Venice*. England's Jews were expelled from the country in 1290 and not allowed back until Cromwell's invitation in the seventeenth century. Possibly some crypto-Jews remained in England, but this has not been proven.

Two reasons compelled me to write a Shakespearean-type narration of the Exodus story. The mundane mechanical reason is that, more than any other individual, Shakespeare was responsible for creating the modern English language, which is, of course, my left and right hands. Secondly, as critic Harold Bloom stated so boldly, Shakespeare invented the human. In his 38 plays and his poetry, he articulated the way we see ourselves. These two facts are enough cause to bow in the Bard's direction while we celebrate our festival of freedom.

All the parts are roughly equal in number of lines, except the three witches have just one short scene. The script is crowded with footnote-citations. It seemed like the right thing to do.

PHARAOH
COUNSELOR
(PHARAOH'S) DAUGHTER
MAID
MOSES
AARON
VOICE
THREE WITCHES

Prologue[1]

VOICE

Two nations, both alike in dignity,
In ancient Egypt, where we lay our scene,
The one upon the next imposed slavery,
With harsh oppression did their lives demean.
The chief defenders of these two foes,
The Pharaoh and the prophet, pledged their life;
To them the seder's story owes
Its lasting theme: redemption's birth in strife.
O such a thriller this romance is,
Though dinner's waiting on the stove!
Well, no, not really. But, perchance, 'tis
A tale that Shakespeare could improve.
Let's do it, then! A play's the best of bids
To catch the full attention of the kids.

DAUGHTER

Friends, Romans, countrymen, lend me your ears.[2]
I could a tale unfold whose lightest word would
harrow up thy soul.[3] However, give it a chance,
because everything finally works out. All's well
that ends well. Here's the Pharaoh in his palace.

PHARAOH

Counselor, I'm contemplating the children of Israel
who arrived in Egypt long ago. Why are they here?

COUNSELOR

Mighty Pharaoh, their ancestor Joseph saved our
people from a terrible famine. He was invited to
bring his family here so that they, too, would not
starve.

PHARAOH   Methinks they still have a lean and hungry look. Also, they think too much. Such men are danger-ous.[4]

COUNSELOR   There sure are a lot of them.

PHARAOH   True, the Israelite people are also too numerous for us. Let us deal shrewdly with them, so that they may not increase.

COUNSELOR   But why, great Pharaoh, would you fear the Israel-ites? They seem peaceful enough.

PHARAOH   Present fears are less than horrible imaginings.[5]   In the event of war, they may join our enemies.

COUNSELOR   *(mildly)* That seems a little paranoid, if you ask me, sir.

PHARAOH   Of all base passions, fear is the most accursed.[6] Look, you want a story or not?

COUNSELOR   Forgive me, Your Highness. So, how would you like to deal shrewdly with them? Do you think we might tame them?

PHARAOH   When I want a straight line, I'll ask for it. Mean-while, my plan is to enslave all the Hebrews, and have all their baby boys thrown into the Nile.

COUNSELOR   Into the Nile? That seems kind of harsh. Consider the litigation.

PHARAOH   All right. That shall be the second thing we do.

COUNSELOR   What's the first thing we do?

PHARAOH   Let's kill all the lawyers![7]

***

DAUGHTER   Come, come, foolish maid, isn't your washing at an end?

MAID	It's this one gown, royal mistress. This wine-stain resists all my efforts. Out, out, damned spot![8]
DAUGHTER	Have you rubbed the stain against a river stone, silly maid?
MAID	Like this?
DAUGHTER	With more gusto, my dim-witted one?
MAID	More like this?
DAUGHTER	Aye, there's the rub![9]
MAID	Noble mistress! Do you see that basket drifting down the river?
DAUGHTER	Make haste to seize it, dullish girl, before it disappears among the reeds.
MAID	It's a baby, bountiful mistress!
DAUGHTER	Quick, check under its garment, and tell me if it is a beautiful girl.
MAID	Alas, mistress, it is a boy.
DAUGHTER	Look closer, stupid girl.
MAID	It is a Jewish boy, royal mistress. Where can his parents be? Should I ask around?
DAUGHTER	No point in that. I'll just keep him myself. I had rather adopt a child than beget it.[10]
MAID	You'll need a nurse, then. Why not ask that little girl over there to find you one?
DAUGHTER	If you think it's necessary.
MAID	Hath not a baby organs, senses, appetites?[11] If you miss his two o'clock feeding, will he not scream to wake the mummies of your ancestors in their tombs?

DAUGHTER   Good point.   Little girl, go find me a Hebrew woman to nurse this child.   If you have a good sense of irony, find his own mother for the job.

***

MOSES   Dear brother, I am fortune's fool.[12]

AARON   In what way, Moses?

MOSES   I have slain an Egyptian who was beating a slave of our house.

AARON   We have slaves in the house?

MOSES   No, our house.   The House of Israel.   I hid the taskmaster's body in the sand.   But I fear I have done but greenly in hugger-mugger to inter him.[13]

AARON   Woe to the hand that shed this costly blood![14]

MOSES   Aaron, come on, the guy was about to kill a helpless slave, one of our tribe!

AARON   That's different.   But you had best flee, or the Pharaoh will doom you to death.   Or, worse, the Pharaoh will doom *me* to death, for not dooming *you* to death.

MOSES   I need a drink.   Where's the nearest apothecary?

***

MOSES   That's odd.   Someone has lit a bush afire.   Even odder, it does not appear to be burning up.

VOICE   Moses!

MOSES   I fear I am not in my perfect mind.[15]   I think it speaks.

VOICE   I am thy father's spirit.[16]

MOSES   Dad? *(pause)* Wanna have a catch?

VOICE	Most foul![17]
MOSES	Sorry about that. It's from hanging out all day with these sheep.
VOICE	Not the sheep, Moses. The foul crimes done in my days of nature.[18]
MOSES	What foul crimes, Dad?
VOICE	Look, forget the Dad thing, okay? It was a meta-phor.
MOSES	So, what are you called?
VOICE	Ehyeh-asher-ehyeh. I shall be what I shall be.
MOSES	Okay – what foul crimes?
VOICE	The enslavement of My people, the Hebrews.
MOSES	Well, you see, all occasions do inform against me. They spur my dull revenge.[19]
VOICE	It's not really about revenge, Moses. I want you to go to Pharaoh and make him let My people go.
MOSES	Wait a minute, wait a minute. That's a job for a great leader. I can't possibly do it. I'm just an ordinary shepherd.
VOICE	Some are born great, some achieve greatness, and some have greatness thrust upon them.[20] You'd be in that last group.
MOSES	To be a king stands not within the prospect of belief.[21]
VOICE	You're not destined to be a king, Moses. This isn't a Scottish play.
MOSES	O God, that one might read the book of fate![22]
VOICE	Well, after a few lessons with a bar-mitsva tutor,

you can! But I can tell you this much now: you're going to be the great prophet of an immortal people.

MOSES   I suppose that's better than spending the rest of my life with these sheep. So, what should I do?

VOICE   Go to Pharaoh and plead with him. Tell him, "Let My people go."

MOSES   How am I supposed to say that?

VOICE   Speak the speech, I pray you, as I pronounced it to you, trippingly on the tongue.[23]

MOSES   Pharaoh won't listen to me. I am slow of speech. I am no orator, as Brutus is.[24]

VOICE   Brutus isn't available, so I'll send along your brother Aaron.

MOSES   Okay, then. Here goes nothing.

***

COUNSELOR Mighty Pharaoh, a shepherd and his brother are here to see you.

AARON   Pharaoh, hear me for my cause.[25] Let the Israelites go, or God will bring a plague upon your house.

PHARAOH   My house? Which house?

AARON   What do you mean, which house?

PHARAOH   I'm a Pharaoh, you moron. You think I have but one house? Get real.

AARON   Yeah? Then, a plague on *both* your houses.[26] A plague on *all* your houses. Heck! *Ten* plagues on all your houses!

***

ALL WITCHES	Double, double, toil and trouble. Fire burn and cauldron bubble.
1ST WITCH	River of blood and sea of frogs!
2ND WITCH	Lice and pests from swamps and bogs!
3RD WITCH	Scourge of beasts and blighted crop.
1ST WITCH	Sorest boils all red on top.
2ND WITCH	Hail and locusts fill the skies.
3RD WITCH	Darkness comes, the firstborn dies.
ALL WITCHES	Double, double, toil and trouble. Fire burn and cauldron bubble.[27]

***

PHARAOH	This is the night that either makes me or foredoes me quite.[28] You Hebrews! Be gone! Stand not upon the order of your going, but go at once![29]
COUNSELOR	Pharaoh, are you really freeing the slaves? Do you repent your treatment of the Hebrew people?
PHARAOH	I have done a thousand dreadful things as willingly as one would kill a fly – and nothing grieves me heartily indeed, but that I cannot do ten thousand more.[30]
COUNSELOR	Do I understand you correctly …?
PHARAOH	If one good deed in all my life I did, I do repent it from my very soul.[31]
COUNSELOR	Yeah, I heard it right. Hey, Hebrews! Wait up for me!

***

MOSES	Aaron! Aaron! I just heard. The Pharaoh will let the slaves go!

AARON	Are you certain, Moses? Possibly he was only joking.
MOSES	Pharaoh, joking? Alas, poor Pharaoh. I know him, Aaron. Not exactly a fellow of infinite jest.[32]
AARON	Then we'd better get moving. If it were done when 'tis done, then 'twere well it were done quickly[33].
MOSES	Wait a bit. There are preparations to be made.
AARON	We're ready. We've already sacrificed a lamb, and put its blood on all the doorways.
MOSES	Was one lamb enough?
AARON	Yes. Who would have thought the old lamb to have had so much blood in him?[34] All right, everyone, get ready to move, and don't even wait for the dough to rise.
MOSES	By which route should we travel?
AARON	Well - there's the long route, by land. Or the shorter route, by sea, direct to Israel.
MOSES	By sea, or not by sea?[35] That is the question.
AARON	Though the seas threaten, they are merciful.[36] Okay, everyone! We're going to walk right through the Red Sea. Hey, Moses! Will you just look at that! The sea is parting!
MOSES	I have mixed feelings about that.
AARON	You do?
MOSES	Parting is such sweet sorrow.[37]
AARON	Too easy, Moses. Hey, the Egyptians are following us!
PHARAOH	What dreadful noise of water in mine ears![38]

MOSES   The sea is closing in on the Egyptians. Friend or brother, he forfeits his own blood that spills another.[39]

COUNSELOR   What's going on? Where's the Pharaoh?

AARON   Full fathom five the Pharaoh lies.[40]

MOSES   But, look, we've arrived at the far side of the Red Sea in safety. We made it!

AARON   We must give thanks to God.

MOSES   But how, where? We have no house of worship. We have no shul.

AARON   We don't need one. All the world's a shul.

MOSES   And the men and women?

AARON   Merely pray-ers.[41]

***

DAUGHTER   My goodness, what an incredible escape. I'm absolutely exhausted. And hungry. Someone pass me the matza.

COUNSELOR   These events should be commemorated in the future. Every year, let us sit upon the ground and tell sad stories of the death of kings.[42]

MAID   I'd rather sit in a chair and lean on a pillow, if it's all the same to you.

AARON   Moses, our people would do well to repeat the tale to their children in the future. This story shall the good man teach his son.[43]

MOSES   We'll make it an official celebration. He that shall live this day, and see old age, will yearly on the vigil feast his neighbors.[44]

DAUGHTER   *He* will feast his neighbors? You mean, his *wife* will feast his neighbors. Understand that you're talking about two days of cooking, on top of a week of cleaning.

AARON   How many ages hence shall this, our lofty scene, be acted over, in states unborn and accents yet unknown?[45]

COUNSELOR   You mean the sad stories of the death of kings, right?

MOSES   It's more than just a story. This is a lesson about living a holy life. Our God is a liberator. To make our existence sacred, we must always resist tyranny, and also resist being tyrants ourselves. How can tyrants safely govern home?[46]

COUNSELOR   And it's not exactly sad, either. It teaches us to treasure what we have. May it be in our flowing cups freshly remember'd.[47] Let's all cry, "Peace, freedom and liberty!"[48]

MOSES   I prefer, "Next year in Jerusalem!"

---

[1] *Romeo and Juliet,* prologue.
[2] *Julius Caesar,* III,ii,80.
[3] *Hamlet,* I,v,15.
[4] *Julius Caesar,* I,ii,201-202.
[5] *Macbeth,* I,iii,137.
[6] *Henry VI, Part One,* V,ii,18.
[7] Ibid, IV,ii,37.
[8] *Macbeth,* V,i,38.
[9] *Hamlet,* III,i,66.
[10] *Othello,* I,iii,189. Orig. *I had rather adopt a child than get it.*

[11] *The Merchant of Venice,* III,i,58. Orig. *Hath not a Jew hands, organs, dimensions, senses, affections, passions?*
[12] *Romeo and Juliet,* III,i, 138.
[13] *Hamlet,* IV,v, 83.
[14] *Julius Caesar,* III,i, 279.
[15] *King Lear,* IV,vii, 63.
[16] *Hamlet,* I,v,9.
[17] Ibid, I,v,27.
[18] Ibid, I,v,30.
[19] Ibid, IV,iv,32.
[20] *Twelfth Night,* II,v,143.
[21] *Macbeth,* I,iii,73.
[22] *Henry IV, Part Two,* III,i,45.
[23] *Hamlet,* III,ii,1.
[24] *Julius Caesar,* III,ii,228.
[25] Ibid, III,ii,13.
[26] *Romeo and Juliet,* III,i,108.
[27] *Macbeth,* IV,i,10-21.
[28] *Othello,* V,i,128-129.
[29] *Macbeth,* III,iv, 118-119.
[30] *Titus Andronicus,* V,i,141.
[31] Ibid, V,iii,189.
[32] *Hamlet,* V,i,185-186.
[33] *Macbeth,* I,vii,1-2.
[34] Ibid, V,i, 42. Orig. *Yet who would have thought the old man to have had so much blood in him?*
[35] *Hamlet,* III,i,56.
[36] *The Tempest,* V,i,178.
[37] *Romeo and Juliet,* II,ii,184.
[38] *Richard III,* I,iv, 22.
[39] *Timon of Athens,* III,v,87.
[40] *The Tempest,* I,ii,397.
[41] *As You Like It,* II,vii,139. Orig. *All the world's a stage, and all the men and women merely players.*
[42] *Richard II,* III,ii,155.
[43] *Henry V,* IV,iii,58.
[44] Ibid, IV,iii,47-48.
[45] *Julius Caesar,* III,i,121-123.

[46] *Henry VI, Part Three,* III,iii,69.
[47] *Henry V,* IV,iii,57.
[48] *Julius Caesar,* III,i,120.

The Lambshank Redemption

At the time I thought of it, *The Lambshank Redemption* seemed like a pretty cool parody title. I still think so, but apparently other people thought of it too. They, however, are mostly restaurant bloggers. What the title said to me, when it first jumped into my head, was, "Guess I have to write a Shawshank parody."

The wonderful 1994 movie *The Shawshank Redemption*, directed by Frank Darabont and based on a novella by Stephen King, presents themes which are strongly connected with the Biblical Exodus. The clash of right against wrong. The human longing for freedom. The terrible responsibilities of assuming control of one's own destiny. It is a lovesong to the blessing of liberation, and so is our seder.

Another thing that links the film and the sacred text is the rejection of moral relativism. Unjust imprisonment, slavery, is immoral in every age, in every place. Resistance to tyranny is part of the design of the human spirit, and our festival reenactment inspires us to recommit to enlarging the circle of freedom so that it encompasses the world.

Red and Andy are the major characters, and the Female Voice, Ramses and Aaron, less so.

RED
ANDY (RABAYNU)
RAMSES
AARON (THE LIBRARIAN)
VOICE (FEMALE)

VOICE   Ladies and gentlemen, you've heard all the evidence, you know all the facts. Witnesses have placed the accused, Andy Rabaynu, at the scene of the crime. A taskmaster is dead. His body was hidden in the sand. And his murder was witnessed by two impeccable Hebrew slaves.

You people are all decent, God-fearing folks. You know that this defendant deserves the maximum punishment allowed by Egyptian law: a lifetime of slavery in a maximum-security penitentiary.

RED   That's how it began for my friend Andy Rabaynu. He ended up just one of the hundreds of thousands of Hebrews, descendants of Jacob, oppressed with hard labor under the cruel hand of the Pharaoh. Just like me.

We all work out our own ways to deal with servitude. This story is about how Andy dealt with it. He was a special kind of man.

Me, on the other hand, I'm not too special. I'm Red C. You can call me Red. There's a slave like me in every Bronze Age civilization, I guess. I'm the guy who can get it for you. From time to time, I've been known to locate scarabs, olive oil, ivory, damn near anything, within reason. Yes, sir, I'm a regular first-dynasty Sears Roebuck.

So when Andy Rabaynu came to me in 1244 B.C.E. and asked me to smuggle a papyrus poster of Cleopatra into Lambshank for him, I told him no problem. And it wasn't.

Andy came to Lambshank Prison in 1247 for murdering a taskmaster who was beating a slave. On the outside, he'd been the adopted son of a Pharaoh's daughter. It was a nice gig for an eighty-year-old man. But now, things couldn't be more different.

RAMSES

I am Mr. Ramses, the Pharaoh of this empire and son of the sun god. You are Hebrews and scum, that's why they sent you here. Rule number one: do as you're told. The other rules you'll figure out as you go along. Any questions?

ANDY

Will you let my people go?

RAMSES

You'll go when we say you go! You eat when we say you eat! You sleep when we say you sleep! Any other questions, you maggot-infected Israelite? No? Good. Welcome to Lambshank.

RED

The first night's the toughest, no doubt about it. When those bars slam home and you're faced with that big old pile of bricks and straw, you know it's for real. Nothing left but all the time in the world to think about it.

ANDY

Hello. I'm Andy Rabaynu.

RED

The taskmaster-killer?

ANDY

How do you know that?

RED

I keep my ear to the ground.

ANDY

What are you in for?

RED

What everybody else is in here for. Planning to join with Egypt's enemies. But we didn't do it.

ANDY

I understand you're a man who knows how to get things. I wonder if you could get me a shepherd's staff?

RED   I'm known to locate things from time to time. What is it, and why?

ANDY   It's a wooden stick, about seven feet long, with a loop at the end.

RED   You looking to plant it in another taskmaster's skull?

ANDY   No. I was just thinking of taking up billiards.

RED   I'll see what I can do.

I could understand why some of the slaves took him for snobby. He had a quiet way about him. He strolled, like a man in a park without a care or a worry.

But we got along fine. The shepherd's staff arrived not long after, and he told me about what he'd had before Lambshank. He'd been a shepherd. It was a monotonous life. But nowhere near as monotonous as the endless days making bricks to build Egyptian store cities – broken up occasionally by the special assignments that Pharaoh would dream up.

One day Andy broke up the monotony himself.

RAMSES   The roof of the Great Pyramid needs resurfacing. I want you men to get up there and make it shine. I mean shine, I kid you not! I want it done by the time I'm finished figuring out these hieroglyphics.

ANDY   Pharaoh, I could help you out with that.

RAMSES   Are you good with symbols, Rabaynu? Can you understand this?

ANDY   Let's see. This appears to be from a book called the Mishna. It's a spiritual instruction of some kind.

RAMSES   Read me some of it.

ANDY	"In each generation, one must look upon oneself as personally having left Egypt."
RAMSES	It sounds like a code. I got to find out what this thing means or I won't know who's plotting to overthrow my dynasty.
ANDY	I suppose I could do that for you, Pharaoh. I'll translate it all, and I'd only ask four cups of wine apiece for my co-workers. I think a man working outdoors feels more like a man if he can have his bottle of Manischewitz. That's only my opinion.
RED	And that's how it came to pass, that the slaves re-surfacing the pyramids wound up sitting in a row at ten o'clock in the morning, drinking lukewarm Concord grape wine, courtesy of the meanest Pharaoh who ever ruled Egypt.
AARON	Andy! Say, thanks for the wine.
ANDY	My pleasure, Aaron.
AARON	I hear you've been reassigned here to the library. Beats making bricks, don't it?
ANDY	I think the Pharaoh wants me nearby to translate his scrolls.
AARON	This library doesn't have much of a collection.
ANDY	No, it's not very extensive. It's just this rock here?
AARON	Yeah, this rock. It's the Rosetta Stone. Hasn't been checked out for centuries. Wish we had more to read. There won't be much for you to do.
ANDY	I suppose I could spend my time trying to help my fellow slaves.
AARON	Like how?
ANDY	Like trying to get the Pharaoh to let them go.

AARON	It's a waste of time, Andy. The Pharaoh is making a fortune off the slaves' labor. He's not going to let us go. He'd have to hire people.
RED	That's right, Andy. As far as he's concerned, there's only three ways to spend royal funds. More mud. More straw. More taskmasters.
ANDY	Still, I'd like to try. I'll send a plague a week. He can't ignore me forever.
RED	So that's how Andy Rabaynu got started inflicting plagues on the Egyptians. First it was the Nile River; Andy turned it into blood. Then swarms of frogs. Then lice. That wasn't what really pissed off the Pharaoh, though.
AARON	Andy! Andy! What are you doing with that record player?
ANDY	Just wait, Red, you're going to like this.
VOICE	*Day-dayenu, day-dayenu, day-dayenu, dayenu dayenu!*
RED	I have no idea to this day what that Jewish lady was singing about. Truth is, I don't wanna know. I would like to think that she was singing about something so unbelievable that she couldn't bring herself to say it in English.
RAMSES	That's it, Rabaynu! A month in the hole for you!
RED	We passed Andy his shepherd's stick in a laundry bag, while he was in solitary. That way he could inflict the plagues of wild beasts, pestilence and boils. In prison, a man will do almost anything to keep his mind occupied.
ANDY	Red? Think you'll ever get out of here?
RED	Sure. When I got a long white beard like yours.
ANDY	Tell you where I'd go. The Promised Land.

RED   Promised Land?

ANDY   Little place on the Jordan River. You know what
             the old spirituals say about the Jordan? They say
             it's deep and wide. That's where I'd like to finish
             out my life, Red. A little condo right on the beach.
             Buy some worthless old ark and fix it up in case
             they decide to re-make the book of Genesis.

RED   Andy, I don't think I could hack it on the outside.
             Been in Egypt too long – four hundred years! I'm
             an institutional slave now.

ANDY   You underestimate yourself. Red – if you ever get
             out of here, do me a favor. There's this big wilder-
             ness in Midian. You know where Midian is?

RED   There's a lot of wilderness out there.

ANDY   One place in particular. Got a big bush there that's
             burning but isn't being consumed. Promise me,
             Red, if you ever get out, find that spot. At the base
             of that bush you'll find some tablets that have no
             earthly business in Midian. You'll find something
             on those tablets that I want you to have.

RED   What? What's on them?

ANDY   You'll just have to look for that bush and see.

RED   And so Andy kept on sending plagues to the Egyp-
             tians, with each one a request to let his people go.
             The next one was hail. Then locusts, and darkness.
             Each time, the Pharaoh refused his application.

             And after nine plagues failed to convince Ramses,
             Andy decided the Hebrews had been here just
             about long enough.

AARON   Andy, come in here and look at this!

ANDY   What are all these boxes doing here?

AARON   They're all addressed to you, every one.

RED   Lord, what happened? This box is full of bones.

ANDY   It's just a dismantled lamb, Red. We'll need the blood for the doors.

RED   I tell you, the man was talkin' crazy. I was worried, I truly was.

AARON   We should keep an eye on him.

RED   We can't. It's still dark from the ninth plague. What was in the other boxes?

AARON   Just a lot of flat bread.

ANDY   I'm going to pay a few calls now. I'll be back soon.

RED   The next morning, right about the time Egypt's firstborn were having their last breakfast, a Hebrew man strolled into the Ibis Bank of Alexandria. Until that moment, he didn't exist, except in the Torah.

ANDY   My name is Moshe the Prophet. I've come to borrow all your jewelry.

RED   He had all the proper ID. His camel's license, slave certificate, Levite security card. The signature was a spot-on match.

VOICE   I must say we'll be sorry to lose your servitude. I hope you'll enjoy living abroad.

ANDY   Thank you. I'm sure I will.

RED   The Prophet visited nearly a dozen Egyptians that morning. All told, he and the Hebrews blew town with a fortune in jewelry – severance pay for four centuries of slavery. His last stop before leading his people to freedom was the editorial office of the Jewish Publication Society.

VOICE   Good morning, sir, can I help you?

ANDY   I have something for the managing editor.

VOICE   You can wait here for him if you prefer, or else I can give it to him when he's finished his meeting.

ANDY   I'm on my way out of town, so I'd be grateful if you'd get that scroll to him.

RED   At midnight, a great cry arose across Egypt, for there was not a house where the firstborn had not died. Except in Lambshank. Death had not visited the doors marked with blood.

              The slaves were ready to leave. But there was still one big obstacle: that stinking expanse of sewage they call the Red Sea.

AARON   Andy! Is there any magic left in that shepherd's staff?

ANDY   Stall the Pharaoh, Red – I'm going to split the sea so the Hebrews can walk through.

RED   Stall him? How?

ANDY   That Cleopatra papyrus. Okay, we're outta here.

RED   In the year 1238 BCE, Andy Rabaynu, accompanied by 600,000 Hebrew slaves, escaped from Lambshank Prison. All they found of him were some matza crumbs and an old shepherd's stick damn near worn down to the nub.

              In the morning, in addition to all the dead firstborn Egyptians, Pharaoh noticed something else strange: all his jewelry was missing. Soon sirens were screaming up and down the Nile Delta.

RAMSES   I want every man in Lambshank questioned! Start with that friend of Rabaynu! There he is! You! Where are they? They musta said something!

RED   No, sir, they didn't.

RAMSES   Lord! It's a miracle! The Hebrew slaves up and vanished like a shofar blast in the wind! Left nothing but some damn horseradish and that cupcake on the wall!

RED   Sir, it's just a poster Andy put up over his door.

RAMSES   Well, I'm ripping her down! *(pause)* What's that?

RED   It's lamb's blood.

RAMSES   Lamb's blood! You mean like the Nile River? So he's led them all to the sea! Men, we're going out after them!

RED   By this time, the Hebrews had reached the water's edge. Andy had raised his shepherd's staff over the sea, and it split in two, leaving a dry path for the escaping slaves. But it wouldn't hold for long. The Hebrews had to decide what to do mighty quick. Get busy walking, or get busy drowning. There ain't nothing in between.

The Pharaoh and his army didn't last too long after that. They walked into the water and were never seen again.

The next day, the whole story was in the Torah. Right there between Genesis and Leviticus, for all the world to see. I left Lambshank soon after. Wasn't nobody there to stop me. I just walked out, into freedom. And, you know, I had no idea what that means. The only clue I had was ...

ANDY   Remember, Red – the burning bush. The wilderness in Midian.

RED   I wandered around for what seemed like years. Decades. There were times it was just me and the harsh truth: no way I'm gonna make it on the outside. I could not remember how to be a free man. Maybe some birds aren't meant to be let out of the cage. Those were the times I felt like going back to Lambshank. The only thing that stopped me – a promise I made to Andy.

But I was so alone, and it was so hot out there. So terribly hot.

VOICE   *(clears throat)*

RED   What? Who was that?

VOICE   I think I heard you say that you're terribly hot.

RED   I – yes – I'm hot. It's hot out here, because it's the desert.

VOICE   There's another reason.

RED   What's that?

VOICE   Well, there's a burning bush right behind you.

RED   Sure enough, I turned around and I was face-to-face with a bush that was burning, but not being consumed.

Uh – thank you. Could I ask – where are you?

VOICE   Look down.

RED   And there I saw a double stone tablet, polished so brightly that it shone. There were words carved on it. I recognized the lettering of my old friend Andy. "Don't steal," it said. "Don't murder. Don't bear false witness." The laws of a free people. I stood there wondering if there was any hope for an old slave like me.

ANDY   Red, hope is a good thing. Maybe the best of things. It gives you the courage to seek freedom. To draw the circle of liberation around everyone. And no good thing ever dies.

VOICE   Red – look over there. That mountain.

RED   I looked, and sure enough, there was a mountain, and a vast crowd of people stood by it, looking up.

VOICE   You should hurry, if you want to catch up with them.

RED   And that's when I finally felt it. The excitement that only a free man can feel, a free man at the start of a long journey whose conclusion is uncertain. A man on the way to the Promised Land. Wherever that might be.

ANDY   Think you could help us find it?

RED   I'm known to locate things from time to time.

The Hitchhiker's Guide to the Exodus

— a Douglas Adams play —

The Hitchhiker's Guide to the Galaxy, a 1979 comic science fiction novel by the late Douglas Adams, is a cult favorite. I include myself in that cult. Its style, liberated from any sense of reality, is a triumph of free association but also a thoughtful exposition about Why The World Happened and Why Are We Here. The book begins, oddly, with the destruction of planet Earth, and then circles back round to its salvation, all the while guided by Ecclesiastes-like advice not to think too hard and to try to enjoy your life.

For me, the *Hitchhiker's Guide* is a challenge to arbitrariness. It's rife with random events, but its protagonists are impelled to find order and meaning in those events and to impose some sort of justice upon them. This is the function of a moral being – to discern patterns and, if not always to understand them, at least to act upon them with integrity.

Douglas Adams emphasized his strong feelings about the value of the individual by presenting a faceoff between a solitary person against an amoral bureaucracy, and then a solitary planet against an unfeeling intergalactic empire. In this way, he affirmed the Torah civil laws which assume the equality of humans, the powerless and the regal. The Hebrew Bible was groundbreaking in its time, when it gave impartiality the force of law.

In our play, Moses and his brother and sister are confronted by a massive injustice and constrained by their own inertia. It requires a powerful force to shake them into action and resist the power-wielders. What is that force?

It doesn't really matter.

All the roles are roughly equal in terms of the number of lines. I didn't actually count them. Why bother? What's the point?

(GUIDE) VOICE
MOISHE DENT
EHYEH (ASHER-EHYEH)
AARVIN (THE DEPRESSED KOHEN)
MILIAM
(PHARAONIC VOGYPTIAN) JELTZ

VOICE   Far beneath uncharted sands in an undiscovered quadrant of northeastern Africa, lie the ashes of a kingdom once known as Vogypt. This kingdom has – or rather had – a problem, which was this: most of the people living there were unhappy for pretty much all the time. This was because they were slaves. And what made their situation massively worse was the fact that they were enslaved by the Vogyptians, the most sadistic carbon-based units that had ever occupied the planet Earth in a three-dimensional way.

These slaves had arrived in that quadrant four hundred years before this story begins, according to the book of Exodus, which is actually the main character. But one can never be quite sure about the four-hundred year figure. It has been debated endlessly by scholars across the galaxy.

EHYEH   Time is an illusion. Lunchtime, doubly so.

VOICE   Nonetheless, the situation of the slaves figures conspicuously in the story, because of an accident that almost didn't happen which freed them from the Vogyptians.

These unfortunate slaves, known by their descendants as Hebrews, had a dreadfully hard life. In addition to their obligation to construct useless artifacts which would be used to decorate the British Museum some time thence, their minds also were confined. They were not allowed to think. When they did, fierce shovel-like creatures would leap out of the sand and smack them in the face. These parasitic creatures fed on curiosity, which begs us to question why they would attack their source of sustenance. But the answer cannot be found without Deep Thought, and the Hebrews had absolutely no time for that. The Vogyptians, who *did* have time, couldn't care less.

We must begin this story with a young lady named Miliam.

MILIAM   ... eight, nine, ten. All right then, I've made ten bricks. So I'll just wrap them up, take them to the building site, and call it a day. Aarvin! Aarvin, can you help?

AARVIN   Ghastly. Look at those bricks. Ironic, aren't they? Wrapped in papyrus that says, "All these bricks have been constructed with a sunny disposition. It is our pleasure to assist in the building of Pithom and Ramses. Have a nice day."

MILIAM   Aarvin, I just need a little help taking them to the work site.

AARVIN   All right. Come on. I guess I have to take you bricks to the work site. Here I am, high priest of the world's first ethical monotheistic civilization, and I have to take bricks to the work site. Call that job satisfaction? 'Cos I don't. Why bother? What's the point?

MILIAM   It's no good dragging everyone else down, Aarvin. We're slaves. That's life.

AARVIN   Life? Don't talk to me about life. God, I'm so depressed.

VOICE   At this exact same time, not far from Vogypt, in a pub in a small suburb in Midian, sat a nondescript shepherd behind a glass of microbrew. Although much later a considerably large group of nonthinkers would deny it strenuously, this shepherd was descended from a proto-human being that had been extinct for millions of years. More to the point, so was Miliam. And Aarvin. The three were, in fact, brothers and sister.

VOICE   Time, gentlemen.

MOISHE   Time? It's not even noon.

VOICE   True, but we're closing early today, before the pub burns down.

MOISHE   What would make you think the pub's about to burn down?

VOICE   Well, the shrubbery's already gone up, so it's reasonable to assume the pub is next.

MOISHE   The shrubbery – ? Oh, right, look at that. It's all in flames. That's unusual. I'm going outside to have a look.

EHYEH   Hello, Moishe.

MOISHE   What?

EHYEH   Look, are you busy?

MOISHE   Well, I have sheep to watch, but other than that, no. Who's speaking, please?

EHYEH   I am Ehyeh-Asher-Ehyeh. The Initial Creator and the God of your ancestors.

MOISHE   Pleased to meet you, I'm sure. I had no idea the Initial Creator was a shrubbery.

EHYEH   It is merely a botanical matrix, Moishe. I am unknowable. At this moment I am present to assign you a role in the foundation of a new society.

MOISHE   Hold it, stop right there. In addition to being seriously intimidated, I must state that I have no qualifications whatsoever for this.

EHYEH   I will be with you.

MOISHE   You see, there's a case in point. I have neither flame-proof gear nor a ceramic pot. I can hardly accommodate you. You have the wrong man.

EHYEH   Perhaps I should explain. Before the Vogyptians enslaved the Hebrew people – *your* people – your tribe was on its way to creating an entirely unique civilization. This project began in the garden of Eden, where your ancestors has just worked out the answer to the question, when suddenly an unpleasant encounter with an apple put all on hold, and the Hebrews soon found themselves in Vogypt.

MOISHE   Wait. What was the answer to the question? For that matter, what was the question?

EHYEH   Oh, Moishe, everybody knows the *question*. "Mah nishtana," etc. We can't waste time on this now.

MOISHE   But wait, Ehyeh, what's the answer?

EHYEH   It was only a working answer – it was by no means developed to the point of explanation. The answer is, "Life, the Exodus, and everything." The meaning of *that* can only be worked out by a functioning religious society.

MOISHE   And why do *I* have a role in this?

EHYEH   Because, Moishe, your brain was an organic part of the penultimate configuration of Eden. Your presence is necessary to channel the program.

MOISHE   Don't tell me you want to dissect my brain!

EHYEH   (*patiently*) No, Moishe. You see, that would be *unethical*. That's a large part of the point. That would violate a number of the Ten Commandments.

MOISHE   What are … Never mind, it can wait. So, what am I supposed to do?

EHYEH   You are to return to Vogypt, retrieve the Red Sea Pedestrians, and present them with the blueprint of this new stage of civilization. Stop! Don't say anything. *I* will provide the blueprint.

MOISHE   Now, pardon me for asking, but exactly how does one go about retrieving 600,000 slaves from the Vogyptians who don't want to part with them?

EHYEH   Ah! Glad you asked. You will have several useful items at your disposal. One is the starship the Heart of God, powered by the prototype Infinite Improbability Drive. You will impress the Vogyptians by turning their rivers to blood, striking down all their livestock simultaneously with disease, blotting out their sun, and splitting the Red Sea.

MOISHE   Yes, I believe I *will* need an Infinite Improbability Drive, at the least. Won't I have to face the Pharaonic Vogyptian Jeltz at some point? I'm terrified of him. And I don't even speak Vogyptian.

EHYEH   Your brother Aarvin will explain all that to you. Don't forget to pick him up on the way. Oh, I nearly forgot. Take this. It's the Hitchhiker's Guide to the Exodus. All the information is digitalized on several trillion microchips, but do read what I wrote on the cover in big, friendly letters.

MOISHE   *(reading)* "Don't Eat Hametz"?

EHYEH   Right. As for understanding the Vogyptian language – no worries. Just stick this piece of gefilte fish in your ear.

MOISHE   Of course. Makes perfect sense.

EHYEH   Yes. Here's your starship! Have a nice trip. Don't forget, I will always be with you.

MOISHE   Just a minute! I have a brother?

VOICE   Probably within microseconds – the Torah is noto-
                riously unspecific about time – Moishe was joined
                by his brother Aarvin on the starship Heart of God.
                Moishe, how are you feeling at this point?

MOISHE   Completely unprepared. And slow of speech.

VOICE   And you, Aarvin?

AARVIN   Hopeless and paranoid.

VOICE   And why is that?

AARVIN   Because this mission has practically zero chance of
                success.

VOICE   Ah, I see the problem. You haven't calculated in
                the effects of Infinite Probability. Step over to that
                console and raise your staff above it. After that,
                please consult your Guide to the Exodus, as I am
                returning to my narrative role.

MILIAM   Two to the power of 613,956 against and falling.

MOISHE   (*alarmed*) What's that?!

AARVIN   Who knows. Sounded like a measurement of im-
                probability.

VOICE   We're dealing with the book of Exodus, so natu-
                rally the improbability factor will be quite robust.
                As a matter of fact, outside the spaceship window,
                an enormous statue of Confucius made entirely of
                pineapple was floating freely while singing "Bei
                Mir Bist Du Schoen." Oh, it just exploded.

AARVIN   There are Hebrew letters on my tunic. I think I'm
                turning into a dreidl. This is exceedingly unpleas-
                ant. I want to go back to Vogypt.

MILIAM   Please do not be alarmed. You are bound to feel some minor ill effects as the improbability factor de-escalates. We are now cruising at a level of two to the power of 12,387 to one against. Normality will be restored as soon as the slaves are freed from Vogypt. Thank you.

MOISHE   I'm still feeling quite unsure of myself. Definitely not a condition in which to approach the Pharaonic Vogyptian Jeltz.

MILIAM   This is easily rectified. Do you know where your towel is?

MOISHE   My towel? Well – we're in the Middle East. My towel is on my head.

MILIAM   Please remove your towel, cut a hole in the middle, and put your head into the hole.

MOISHE   Okay then. Done it. Wait, what are these fringes at the corners?

MILIAM   Those are your tsitsit. They are reminders of your purpose, and will assist you in your attempts to channel Deep Thought.

MOISHE   And that would be – ?

AARVIN   Deep Thought, Moishe, come on, where have you *been?* Deep Thought is the moral force of the universe. You conduct the moral energy waves when you apply pure intention to the tsitsit. Honestly, I don't understand how we could be related.

MOISHE   You're the High Priest, Aarvin, you can't expect everyone else to know these things.

MILIAM   We are now at a level of 3489 to one against.

MOISHE   That's quite a nice boost, isn't it? I'm beginning to feel positively optimistic.

AARVIN   You pathetic maniac.

VOICE	The Heart of God has entered Vogyptian airspace, and lands near a crater formed by the impact of a collapsing autocracy.
EHYEH	Now, Moishe, when you approach the Pharaonic Vogyptian Jeltz, remember that I am with you. Also the fate of a brilliant civilization. Keep your towel on and don't lose your nerve.
JELTZ	Another spacecraft. This one's pink. Hullo, two gnomish little men! I just want to make it totally clear that you are not welcome.
MOISHE	Pharaonic Jeltz, I have come to ask you to let my people, the Hebrew slaves, go.
JELTZ	Ah, yes, well, I'm afraid there's little chance of that. As you are no doubt aware, the plans for development of the Vogyptian dynastic empire require the participation of six hundred thousand slaves, and your people, as you call them, are they.
MOISHE	But, Pharaonic Jeltz, the Initial Creator has sent us to free the slaves so that they may ... well, I'm not totally clear about what they're to do afterwards, but they're going to become a brilliant civilization.
JELTZ	I worked hard to get where I am today, and I didn't become Pharaonic Vogyptian simply so I could set free a bunch of shiftless Hebrew slaves. So, get lost. I've just had an unhappy love affair, and I don't see why anybody else should have a good time. And, by the way, I can tell you're not from this quadrant. How did you learn to understand Vogyptian?
MOISHE	I have a piece of gefilte fish in my ear.
JELTZ	That's terrific. Now, get lost. There will be no freedom for the slaves.
MOISHE	But that's not fair.

JELTZ   Not fair, is it? You were quite entitled to make any suggestions or protests at the appropriate time, you know. The plans have been available in the local planning office for the past nine millennia.

AARVIN   Of course. They were on display inside a Middle Kingdom sarcophagus in a disused chamber in a pyramid in Giza, with a sign on the door reading "Beware of the Sphinx."

JELTZ   That's all quite irrelevant now.   I will not let the slaves go.

MOISHE   Then I'm sorry to say that we will have to reveal the power of the Almighty. Aarvin?

JELTZ   How remarkable. A bowl of petunias hovering in the air – in much the same way that bricks don't.

VOICE   Oh, no, not again.

AARVIN   Dear me. Sorry about that.

JELTZ   Somebody get in here and clean this up. You two Hebrews – you don't impress me, and you smell of sheep. Get out.

MOISHE   Pharaonic Jeltz, your kingdom will be afflicted with plagues. The combined forces of nature will rise up and compel you to let the slaves go free.

JELTZ   Really, now. What are the odds of that?

MILIAM   We are now at a probability factor of one to one, and holding.

JELTZ   Is that supposed to frighten me? You make me laugh. Resistance is useless. What's that screaming outside?

AARVIN   I would guess that the Nile River has turned to a liquid that is almost, but not quite, entirely unlike blood. And, that all the frogs in it have fled ashore as a consequence.

JELTZ   Blood I understand, but frogs? I mean, that doesn't even make any sense as a metaphor. They're just ridiculous creatures hopping around.

MOISHE   The frogs are not quite as they appear. They are the protrusion into our consciousness of hyperintelligent, pan-dimensional beings. The whole business with the hopping and croaking is just a front.

JELTZ   Well, they're not as hyperintelligent as I. And I won't let the slaves go. And you can go ... my goodness, I'm itching something terrible.

MOISHE   That would be the plague of lice.

AARVIN   You'd better close the windows.

JELTZ   Why? It's a lovely spring day ... Great Vogon, is that a penguin?

AARVIN   It is, and if you don't close your windows you'll be overrun with wild beasts.

JELTZ   This is somewhat unnerving. Servants, instruct the people to lock up the livestock.

VOICE   Too late, Your Eminence. The cattle have all expired of a curious disease.

MOISHE   The Almighty says, with a mighty arm I will force the Pharaonic Jeltz to let the Hebrews go free.

JELTZ   A mighty arm, is it? Well, here's *my* mighty arm ... bloody hell, it's covered with boils!

MOISHE   Will you let them go?

JELTZ   No! I will *not* let them go!

MOISHE   What?

JELTZ   I *said*, I will not let them go! What's that awful clattering? I can't hear myself think.

AARVIN   Have you got a tin roof on this palace?

JELTZ   A tin roof? Yes.

AARVIN   That would explain it. Hail.

MOISHE   By this point, Pharaonic Jeltz, one would think you'd realize that the combined forces of nature have – well, have *combined.*

JELTZ   A mere annoyance. Slave, wave that palm fan with a bit more energy, please – it's hot in here.

AARVIN   The palm fan informs me that it can no longer function effectively as a cooling device. Its leaves are all gone.

JELTZ   And how did that happen?

AARVIN   They were eaten by these locusts. Can't you see them?

JELTZ   No, I can't see them, since someone's been kind enough to turn out all the lights, you obnoxious bugblat!

AARVIN   I can see this relationship is something we're going to have to work at.

MOISHE   Pharaonic Jeltz, no matter how you feel about the improbability factor, you must acknowledge that a lot of the rules of the physical universe have been broken recently. Nine, in fact. What would be more improbable than these, however, is your persistent delusion that the universe is going to stop pounding you before you free the Hebrew slaves.

JELTZ   For certain, nothing's going to happen till the lights come back on.

AARVIN   You haven't much control over this situation, you know.

JELTZ	I could read you some Vogyptian poetry.
MOISHE	Will you look at that – the darkness is gone.
JELTZ	Get lost, lowly blights on the planet. I never want to see you again.
EHYEH	And you won't. All right, Hebrews, clear out and prepare for the tenth and last affliction on the Vogyptians.
MOISHE	All right, then. I'm far from home, in a hostile environment, and despite epic difficulties wrought upon the Vogyptians, the slaves are still not free. What's next?
EHYEH	*(patiently)* Look at the Hitchhiker's Guide, Moishe.
MOISHE	It says, "Don't eat hametz."
EHYEH	That's right. Don't eat any bread for awhile. And also, put whale's blood on the sides of all the slaves' doors.
MOISHE	Of course. Why didn't I think of that before?
AARVIN	I'm surprised you didn't, actually.
MOISHE	I was being sardonic. So, where am I supposed to get whale's ... Great heavens, what was *that*?
VOICE	It was a whale striking the ground at high velocity. Go on, then, mark all the slaves' doors, and prepare for a rapid exit from Vogypt.
MOISHE	I can't. Really, I can't. I understand about the burning bush and the gefilte fish, but mucking about with whale's blood takes it too far. I feel I may explode if there's any more irrationality.
EHYEH	I quite understand, Moishe. You're a human, after

all. You desire to understand what's going on.

MOISHE   I really do.

EHYEH   Very well. Let's then amend the instruction. In-
            stead of a whale – let's see – oh! A lamb. Lambs
            are sacred to the Vogyptians. Using it to protect
            the Hebrew slaves would be sheer poetry. Great! I
            like it.

MOISHE   All right. This makes a little sense. So, we use the
            blood of a sacrificial lamb –

EHYEH   A *pesaḥ*, we'll call it –

MOISHE   And we mark the Hebrews' doors … oh, wait a
            minute. How will the doors feel about this?

AARVIN   They're bound to object.

EHYEH   Worry not, little friends, the doors have all been
            programmed with cheerful and sunny dispositions.
            It will be their pleasure to assist in the protection of
            the Hebrews from the tenth plague. Aarvin, please
            go instruct them.

AARVIN   I won't enjoy it.

EHYEH   That's fine.

MOISHE   But, Ehyeh, what is this tenth plague? You're mak-
            ing me nervous.

EHYEH   I'm going to use an atomic vector plotter to propel
            all the firstborn of the Vogyptians into a bottle of
            horseradish sauce.

            (Pause.)

MILIAM   That's quite inventive.

MOISHE   And … you feel this will effect the freedom of the
            Hebrew slaves.

EHYEH	It will.
AARVIN	It's more interesting than boils, I suppose.
MOISHE	And then?
EHYEH	I will escort the slaves back to their own proper dimension, and they will re-commence their work of creating a principled civilization. That's it. That's the plan.
MILIAM	I suppose we should get ready to go, then.
EHYEH	Do. Now, on the count of 613, we'll have a last look back at Jeltz.
VOICE	One, two, three, four, 612, 613.
JELTZ	Freddled gruntbuggly! All the firstborn have disappeared! What's to become of my dynastic empire? What am I to do now? My nerves are shot. Slavey, bring me a Pan Galactic Gargle Blaster. I have to think.
AARVIN	This won't end well.
MOISHE	Everyone into the starship, now. No time to lose. You, there, get rid of those Weetabix. Leavening interferes with the navigation software. Are we all inside? Good. Aarvin, power up the thrusters.
JELTZ	Holy beeblebrox, they're leaving on a starship! Energize – aarrggh, what's in this drink? Shoot – it tastes like horseradish, someone get me some water – ugh – there we go – that's better. Now, energize the demolition beams! Shoot it down!
VOICE	But, Pharaonic Jeltz, it's too late. The Heart of God is out of range.
JELTZ	What a rotten day I've had. The slaves have all escaped, and my butler can't make a decent Pan Galactic Gargle blaster.

MILIAM	And apparently you've swallowed all the Vogyptian firstborn.
VOICE	It works in Greek mythology, so why not here?
EHYEH	What about that! There's still a surprise or two left in the universe.
MOISHE	The starship appears to be functioning well. Ehyeh, where are we going, and how long will it take us to get there?
EHYEH	Hard to say exactly. We're about to reach the sea of Damogran. The Heart of God can blast right past that without any problem. From there it's five hundred thousand light-years to our destination.
AARVIN	Without any Weetabix?
EHYEH	Yes. It's quite a minor undertaking when you compare it with your task at the end of this journey. Once arrived, you are charged with forming a just society. A system that works toward the perfection of the world. In fact, your job is to find, and articulate, a way to make human life sacred.
AARVIN	You can leave me out of it.
EHYEH	No, you won't be left out of it. You're the High Priest. You're in charge of ritual. Humans need ritual to pass on their values. There's no alternative to ceremonials, Aarvin.
AARVIN	I predict a great deal of pushback.
EHYEH	Yes, of course people are going to have issues with the physical form of ritual. They'll have to adapt them for their own time. But they can't function without them, so, Aarvin, stay with it and you'll be fine. In fact, there's a terrific costume in it for you.
MILIAM	But, this journey we're on. How do we get to this destination? Can the Heart of God navigate itself?

VOICE   Where's your towel, Moishe?

MOISHE   Here it is. I'm still wearing it. It has fringes on it now.

VOICE   Yes, yes, I know. That's all in the Hitchhiker's Guide to the Exodus. Now, just take those fringes in your hand, and look at them.

MOISHE   Okay.

VOICE   These are your *tsitsit*. Look at them and remember your obligations to bring these people home, and to set them to the task of perfecting the world.

MOISHE   But I don't know ...

EHYEH   Knowledge comes later. What you need now is pure intention. Do you intend to channel all your efforts toward regenerating the Garden of Eden?

MOISHE   *(pause)* Yes. That's my intention.

MILIAM   Great heavens, we're going fast!

VOICE   Well done, Moishe.

AARVIN   Would someone mind telling me what's next?

VOICE   We'll reach our destination in seven or eight days. At our first stop, you can have all the Weetabix you like.

MILIAM   And where will that be?

VOICE   The kosher deli at the end of the universe.

Dial M for Moses

— a Hitchcock play —

What story is more Hitchcockian than the story of Moses? Has an innocent bystander ever been thrust more abruptly into the center of action and intrigue, and impelled by irresistible forces to engage and oppose an evil villain, than Moses?

Alfred Hitchcock never made a biblical epic. Most of his films were set in the present day. *Jamaica Inn* and *Under Capricorn* were exceptions, but those were only set in the 19th century. Had he ever been tempted to venture back in history, it is delightful to ponder what Sir Alfred would have made of the Exodus story.

Just like Guy Haines in *Strangers on a Train*, Father Logan in *I Confess*, Ben McKenna in *The Man Who Knew Too Much*, Roger Thornhill in *North by Northwest*, and Richard Blaney in *Frenzy*, Moses was minding his own business one minute, and the next, fleeing a murder rap, confronting a burning bush, facing off against Pharaoh, delivering plagues, and parting the Red Sea. What a "Good evening!" the Master of Suspense could have created out of that.

As you read *Dial M for Moses*, see how many Hitchcock titles and scene descriptions you recognize. Finding the film references is part of the fun of the play.

MOSES
PASSERBY/BLONDE
1ST ISRAELITE
2ND ISRAELITE
TASKMASTER/ (PALACE) GUARD
VOICE
AARON
PHARAOH

MOSES   *(sings)* "Que sera, sera, whatever will be, will be, the future's not ours to see, que sera, sera, what will be, will be." What a beautiful blue sky. *(shouting)* Hey, you! The ram with the curly horns! Leave that ewe alone! Now, behave yourself! *(normal voice)* That's about all the excitement we'll have today. Being a shepherd is such a peaceful life. No worries, no cares. No one trying to plunge a scissors between my shoulder blades. No ominous music in the background. I'm not even laid up with a broken leg. It's just me and my sheep. Good afternoon, Taskmaster.

TASKMASTER   Good afternoon, Mo – urgh!

MOSES   It's Mo-*ses*. Hey! What happened!? There's a Khopesh sword sticking in your back!

TASKMASTER   *(gasping for breath)* Mo-ses – go to Mi-dian. See bush – burning – burning bush.

MOSES   Bernie Bush? In Midian?

TASKMASTER   *(gasping for breath)* No – bur – *(Dies.)*

PASSERBY   Murder! Murder! That shepherd murdered a taskmaster!

MOSES   No! It wasn't me! Honest – I'm not a murderer, I'm a herderer.

***

MOSES	I can't run anymore. I've got to rest. Hey, that's strange. Someone is plowing a field. But there isn't any field. And he's headed right at me! A passing manure wagon. I'll flag it down. Stop! Help! Watch out for the plow! Oh, God – what a mess! Wait a minute, this is Midian. Excuse me – sir?
PASSERBY	Yes?
MOSES	Do you know someone around here named Bernie? Bernie Bush?
PASSERBY	I know a Bernie Tush. He's at the rear end of town.
MOSES	Maybe I got the name wrong.
VOICE	Oh, Moses.
MOSES	Yes? Who is it? Where are you?
VOICE	Over here.
MOSES	I can't tell where you are. Is that you? The fat guy walking a camel?
VOICE	That's a cameo, not a camel. No. Pay no attention to him, he won't show up again. I'm in this burning bush.
MOSES	Oh, *burning* bush. Now I get it.
VOICE	Listen – I'm sorry about the mix-up with the taskmaster.
MOSES	Well, no one speaks very clearly with a Khopesh sword in his back.
VOICE	No, I mean your being accused of his murder.
MOSES	You know about that? Then you know I had nothing to do with it.
VOICE	I do.

MOSES   You know everything?

VOICE   I know too much.

MOSES   I've been running for so long! And it's really hard to move fast wearing this disguise – my mother's dress and wig.

VOICE   You're safe, Moses. I've been keeping watch over you.

MOSES   From this burning bush?

VOICE   Yes. Why are you staring?

MOSES   I'm spellbound.

VOICE   There's something I need you to do for me.

MOSES   Get a fire hose?

VOICE   Go to Pharaoh, and tell him to let my people go.

MOSES   But I'm a shepherd covered in manure. I'm also slow of speech.

VOICE   So make a deal with your brother, Aaron. He speaks clearly and bathes frequently.

MOSES   My brother? You mean, from my birth family? Why should Aaron agree to do this for me?

VOICE   Because you'll agree to do something he wants *you* to do.

MOSES   I do his job and he does mine? Like what?

VOICE   He helps you with the talking. You help him with the magic.

MOSES   I think I see. Criss-cross.

***

MOSES   Well, this is the Pharaoh's palace all right, but I have no idea how to get in.

GUARD	Hey! You! Come over here!
BLONDE	You'd better hide.
MOSES	Hide? Where?
BLONDE	Here, behind this obelisk.
GUARD	Where'd that guy with the beard go?
BLONDE	He went that way, I think. He said something about catching an express barge for the Valley of the Kings.
MOSES	*(pause)* It looks like the coast is clear. Thank you very much!
BLONDE	Quite all right. What would a palace guard want with you, if I may ask?
MOSES	I have a lot of unpaid camel tickets.
BLONDE	Of course.
MOSES	Heavens, but you're an interesting-looking person. I've never seen anyone with yellow hair before.
BLONDE	It *is* sort of out of place in Egypt, but the director insisted.

(Pause.)

MOSES	I know. I look vaguely familiar to you.
BLONDE	Yes.
MOSES	You feel you've seen my face somewhere before. Perhaps at the movies?
BLONDE	You definitely look notorious. I think you're the man who killed a taskmaster. That's why they're all looking for you.

MOSES   I didn't!   I was there, but someone else killed him.
                Look, I don't have much time to discuss this. You
                don't by any chance know how I can get in to see
                the Pharaoh, do you?

BLONDE   He's inside the palace. If you want to see him, just
                look through this rear window.

MOSES   No, I need to speak to him. A voice in a burning
                bush instructed me to convince Pharaoh to free the
                Hebrew slaves.

BLONDE   Sure it did. You're in luck. I'm on my way into the
                palace to deliver some kohl.   There's a latchkey
                hidden under the stair carpet.   Come with me.
                Hope you're in good condition; there's a very tall
                staircase to climb. Thirty-nine steps.

MOSES   Why, this is very kind of you. Why are you help-
                ing me?

BLONDE   I like men who are slow of speech.

MOSES   Or else I must have one of those faces you can't
                help believing.

                                    ***

AARON   Moses! I've been waiting for you.

MOSES   Aaron! This can't be real! Where were you? I
                didn't see you.

AARON   I was hiding behind that torn curtain.

MOSES   My gosh, how long has it been?

AARON   I haven't seen you since you were a baby, Moses.
                After Mother gave you up for adoption, we lost
                track of you.

MOSES   I never knew why she did that.

AARON   A fake psychic convinced her.   Said you would only survive if you were floated down the Nile River in a basket.

MOSES   It would have been great to know my real parents.

AARON   Yes, especially since you were supposed to be the heir to the family fortune.

MOSES   What fortune?

AARON   I'm not sure myself, but I think there was some promised land involved.

MOSES   A family plot? We can talk about that later. What a beautiful palace. Is that the Pharaoh himself? This must be our lucky day. Pharaoh, I'm Moses. This is my brother Aaron.

PHARAOH   So?

AARON   We have a message for you. Thus says Adonai, God of the Hebrews: let my people go.

PHARAOH   I see no reason to let your people go.

AARON   With a mighty arm, the Lord will bring the slaves out of Egypt into freedom.

PHARAOH   Are you threatening me? I'm warning you both – you're mixed up in something you don't understand.

MOSES   No, Pharaoh, it's you who doesn't understand. Have you ever been attacked by a flock of birds, strangled with a necktie, or had some nut with a knife stab you through a shower curtain?

PHARAOH   No.

MOSES   Then your life is about to get very interesting.

***

GUARD   Pharaoh, I'm tendering my resignation. My psychiatrist told me I can't work here any more. This job is aggravating my phobias. I'm too stressed.

PHARAOH   I relieved you from watch-tower duty. I knew you were afraid of heights. What's your problem now?

GUARD   I'm also afraid of frogs. And wild beasts. And darkness.

PHARAOH   You know, this may surprise you, but I'm very sympathetic. I confess, I can't stand it anymore. First, all our bath water turned to blood. Then birds started pecking at me. Then I got dizzy every time I tried to climb a pyramid. Then everything went dark and I ran out of flashbulbs. And now my first-born son gets kidnapped – and unless someone starts singing "Que Sera, Sera," I'll never find him.

GUARD   Thanks for understanding, Pharaoh. I really need a change of scenery. I'm planning to take a nice long train trip somewhere.

***

1ST ISRAELITE   Where do we go, Moses?

MOSES   To the Red Sea, Harry.

1ST ISRAELITE   Which way is that?

MOSES   North. Well, maybe northwest.

2ND ISRAELITE   Don't you have a map? Harry will get lost.

MOSES   That's the trouble with Harry.

BLONDE   The Red Sea? Is it really red? I can't stand the sight of red.

1ST ISRAELITE   We'd better move faster. I can see them coming after us.

2ND ISRAELITE   The birds? I saw them too.

1ST ISRAELITE	No, the Egyptians.
MOSES	Is everyone here? Do we have all the tribes?
AARON	Oh, we have twelve tribes. Twelve multitudes, twelve tribes.
2ND ISRAELITE	I'm hungry.
MOSES	We've no time to cook anything. Grab a sack of potatoes. Not the sack with the dead body inside, one of the other ones.
2ND ISRAELITE	Harry, I just don't know about this. I don't trust Moses. He could have poisoned the potatoes. He did kill that taskmaster, you know.
1ST ISRAELITE	That doesn't make any sense. Why would he poison us?
2ND ISRAELITE	Just a suspicion. Maybe because we know he's carrying all that Egyptian jewelry.
1ST ISRAELITE	Your imagination is running away with you. But I'm not sure I want to spend eight days every year eating raw potatoes. Moses, I'm just going to bring some sacks of flour. I'd rather eat unleavened bread.
MOSES	As you wish.

***

1ST ISRAELITE	How do we cross the sea, Moses?
MOSES	Didn't anyone bring a lifeboat?
1ST ISRAELITE	No.
MOSES	That's too bad.
2ND ISRAELITE	Say, what happened to that blonde woman?
AARON	Looks like the lady vanished.

2ND ISRAELITE   That's so weird.

AARON   Yes – I don't know what's going on with her.   She isn't quite herself today.

1ST ISRAELITE   Forget her!   The Egyptian army is coming.   We're trapped! We're going to die!

MOSES   Don't get all in a frenzy! Possibly I can part the waters.

2ND ISRAELITE   Part the waters?   Hey, did you hear that, everybody?   Moses says he's going to part the waters! What are you – some kind of psycho?

AARON   Everybody!   Ready to walk through the Red Sea? Moses, hold up your staff over the water!

1ST ISRAELITE   Look!   A dry path through the sea!   We can get through!

AARON   Faster! Here come the Egyptians!

PHARAOH   Get them, men! They have the jewels!

2ND ISRAELITE   Well, would you look over there. The water is closing in on the Egyptians.

AARON   What an unbelievable ending.

1ST ISRAELITE   Do you have any last words, Pharaoh? Are you sorry you enslaved the Hebrews?

PHARAOH   Shall we stand in shallower water and discuss that?

Give My Regards to Pharaoh

— a Broadway musical —

It is beyond dispute that Jews dominated American musical theater for most of its history. Although overtly Jewish themes were absent until *Fiddler on the Roof* in 1964, theater historians have pointed out the ever-present themes of racism, inequality, and the struggles against them that echoed the Jewish experience.

Many of the shows of Oscar Hammerstein II, both before and during his collaboration with Richard Rodgers dealt explicitly with the challenges of multiculturalism; these included *Showboat, South Pacific, The King and I,* and *Flower Drum Song.* In addition, a central theme of *The Sound of Music* was the rise of Nazism. Burton Lane and "Yip" Harburg's *Finian's Rainbow* squarely confronted the issue of racism in the South. Leonard Bernstein and Stephen Sondheim presented a tragic story of anti-immigrant prejudice in *West Side Story.* Class identity and transition is the theme of *My Fair Lady.* There are many others.

Jewish writers chose these themes because they understood them, and, in doing so, created a genre in which songs expressed their deep feelings about their otherness, and the struggle of the outsider. Here on the musical stage, American theater companies described the challenges of a pluralist world.

Give My Regards To Pharaoh uses melodies which are well-known, but perhaps you might glance through the lyrics before the seder to make sure that your singers know in advance how the words fit the music.

I am deeply indebted to Richard Weill for his help with these songs.

GOD
MOSES
AARON
MIRIAM
PHARAOH
(SLAVE) CHORUS

[Melody: "Aquarius" from *Hair*]

MIRIAM
When the Jews were held in slavery
And misery was all you could find
A child came floating in a basket
With freedom not far behind

CHORUS
This is the dawning of the age of the Israelites
The age of the Israelites
The Israelites, the Israelites!

MIRIAM
God is in a bush that's burning
Soon the Pharaoh will be learning
What the plea to let us go meant
Lest the plagues the Lord will foment
Pharaoh may regret he waited
When at last we're liberated

CHORUS
The Israelites, the Israelites!

MIRIAM
When the Pharaoh issued his command
For all to drown the sons of Israel
A man was summoned forth to lead us,
Tonight, we tell his tale.

CHORUS
This is the dawning of the age of the Israelites
The age of the Israelites
The Israelites, the Israelites!
The Israelites, the Israelites!

MIRIAM
Aaron, this has to be the saddest day of my life.

AARON	I feel awful, Miriam. His life has just begun. And we'll probably never see him again.
MIRIAM	We can't hide him any longer. The Egyptians will find him, and they'll throw him in the Nile to drown. Mama said this is the only way to save him.
AARON	Did you line the basket with pitch?
MIRIAM	Yes. There's no way it can sink.
AARON	Well, baby brother – bon voyage.
MIRIAM	We love you, Moses!
AARON	We sure do, little dude.
MIRIAM	I'll walk along the bank and watch you for as long as I can.
AARON	May this river take you far away from slavery.

[Melody: "Ol' Man River" from *Show Boat*]

CHORUS	*Baby Moses*
	The baby Moses
	He must know somethin'
	But don't say nothin'
	He jest keeps floatin'
	His basket's floatin' along
	His sister ganders
	As he meanders
	Through reeds he wanders
	His fate she ponders
	While he keeps floatin'
	His basket floatin' along
	On the banks the Hebrews strain
	Bodies all achin' and wracked with pain
	Pack that straw

Make those bricks
Stop to catch your breath
You get whips and kicks

Pharaoh's daughter
Is by the water
She'll save the baby
So someday maybe
He'll lead his people
To freedom -
Don't take too long!

MOSES   This looks like a good place to rest. I guess the sheep are safe here. There's a creek and ... what on earth is that?! That bush is on fire, but ... but it's not burning up. I have to get a better look at this.

GOD   Moses, Moses!

MOSES   Here I am. Who's – who's speaking? Who are you?

GOD   I am the God of your ancestors, Moses.

MOSES   The God of my ancestors! You mean, the desert god? The river god?

GOD   No, not the gods of the Pharaohs. I am the one true God, who made a covenant with Abraham, Isaac, and Jacob. And I am telling you to go back to Egypt, and tell Pharaoh to free the Hebrew slaves, who are My people.

MOSES   Wait a minute, I can't do that! The Pharaoh won't listen to me!

GOD   With a mighty arm I will compel Pharaoh to free the Hebrews.

MOSES   A mighty arm? I don't see a mighty arm! I just see a burning bush! I don't understand this at all.

GOD   Apparently not.   Moses, stop waffling, and focus!
             This is not how one behaves in the presence of the
             Eternal.

[Melody: "Take Back Your Mink" from *Guys and Dolls*]

GOD   *Take off your shoes!*
             Get on your knees!
             What made you think,
             That I was one of those trees?

             Lay down your staff!
             Don't stand around!
             I'm burning mad,
             And this is sanctified ground.

             I know that you will follow all my decrees,
             Do exactly as I desire.
             Or you will find that I'm not easy to please,
             And like – to set – things on fire.

             So turn up the heat,
             Until Pharaoh melts.
             And bring your brother to help you
             Warn Pharaoh, "Or else!"

MOSES   This is some serious business. I wonder if I'll be
             able to do this.

AARON   Moses, don't worry. I'm here to help.

MOSES   Who are you?

AARON   I'm your brother, Moses. I'm Aaron. I've been sent
             to speak for you to the Pharaoh.

MOSES   My brother?! But you look like a Hebrew!

AARON   I *am* a Hebrew, Moses. So are you. Our sister
             Miriam and I floated you down the Nile River
             when you were a baby, to save your life.

MOSES	This is an awful lot to take in, Aaron. I need some time to digest this.
AARON	We don't have a lot of time. Every day, the slaves are suffering and dying. We need freedom so we can get back to the Promised Land and fulfill our covenant. And the Pharaoh isn't exactly open to suggestion.
MOSES	You're right – I don't remember him being a very nice guy.
AARON	But this is our destiny. This is what we have to do. God is with us.
MOSES	All the same, I'm not looking forward to the next scene.

***

PHARAOH	I'm so tired. It's been such a long day, I'm absolutely bushed. Somebody hit the lights – I'm going to turn in. Oh, no, who's this now? What do you want?
AARON	My name is Aaron, and this is my brother Moses. We've been sent here by the Eternal God to tell you to free the Hebrew slaves.
PHARAOH	Free the slaves, eh? This is a novel approach. Why on earth would I want to do that?
AARON	The Lord our God commands it.
PHARAOH	Oh! The Lord your God commands it! Well, that makes a big difference, doesn't it?
MOSES	I'm glad you see things our way.
PHARAOH	I don't! It was a joke! I was being sarcastic! Now, get lost. I'm tired.
AARON	But will you let our people go?

PHARAOH   There's no earthly reason I should free my slaves.

[Melody: "Gee, Officer Krupke" from *West Side Story*]

AARON   *Dear kindly Mister Pharaoh*
               You do not understand
               God wants us over there so
               We find the Promised Land

MOSES   *We can't be disrespectful*
               We cannot answer, "No!"
               Golly, Pharaoh,
               Let my people go!

PHARAOH   *Gee, Moses and Aaron*
               You've got me all wrong
               The Israelites can leave here
               At the end of this song
               I don't want to hold them
               Or keep them behind
               Though I will often change my mind

CHORUS   *Change my mind!*
               Change his mind, change his mind
               Change his evil mind
               He is often known to change his mind

AARON   *Most wondrous of the Pharaohs*
               You're making a mistake
               Our God is not a joker
               Our God is not a fake

MOSES   *Don't punish all of Egypt*
               Don't bring your country low
               Golly, Pharaoh,
               Let my people go!

PHARAOH   *Gee, Moses and Aaron*
               I've had quite enough
               For no one likes to hear all this belligerent stuff

You say God's almighty,
The plagues God will spew –
Moses and Aaron,
Spew you!

***

MIRIAM   Well, that didn't work out too well.

AARON   No, it didn't. Hope you have some other ideas, Moses.

MOSES   *Ten* other ideas – but they're not actually mine. Plagues upon Egypt!

MIRIAM   Plagues? What are they?

MOSES   Unnatural phenomena that terrify and discomfort.

AARON   Such as?

MOSES   Turning the waters of the Nile into blood. Frogs. Lice. Wild beasts. Things like that.

MIRIAM   Those might be effective. But won't they punish the Hebrews, too?

MOSES   No. God will protect the Hebrews. But Pharaoh will soon know a power greater than his own.

[Melody: "Comedy Tonight" from *A Funny Thing Happened on the Way to the Forum*]

MOSES   *Something that's fright'ning*
Something with lightning
Something for everyone
Another plague tonight

AARON   *Something that's scary*
Something that's hairy
For the unwary there's
Another plague tonight

MIRIAM   *Nothing for Jews*
                No plagues on us
                No need to worry
                No need to fuss

MOSES   *Something that's retching*

AARON   *Something that's kvetching*

MIRIAM   *Something to sap the Pharaoh's might*

ALL   *Liberty tomorrow,*
                Another plague tonight

MOSES   *Something that's falling*

AARON   *Something that's galling*

MIRIAM   *Something for everyone*
                Another plague tonight

MOSES   *Something that's bloody*

AARON   *Something that's muddy*

MIRIAM   *Something for everyone,*
                A plague for every night

AARON   *It's growing dark*
                Can't see a thing
                Can't drink the water
                Thanks to the king

MOSES   *Egypt is reeling*
                Bugs on the ceiling
                Something is cutting off the light
                Liberty tomorrow
                Another plague tonight

AARON   *Something that's fright'ning*
                Something with lightning

Something for everyone
Another plague tonight

MIRIAM   *Something that's scary*
Something that's hairy
Something that's sure to take a bite

MOSES   *Pestilence and hailing*

AARON   *Eczema that's scaling*

MOSES   *Animals that slaughter*

AARON   *Blood in all the water*

MIRIAM   *A swarm of lice*
That's not so nice

MOSES   *A locust blight*
The day turns night

AARON   *And gnats – bats – flies – skies –*
Hocus – pocus – wonder – thunder

MOSES   *Tell all the Jews*
Don't get verklempt
Blood on your doorposts
Makes you exempt

AARON   *Boils that are popping*
Frogs that are hopping
Cattle are dropping out of sight

ALL   *Exodus tomorrow*
Homicide, homicide, homicide, homicide, homicide
Homicide, homicide, homicide, homicide –
Tonight!

***

MOSES   Get the word out as quickly as you can. The Pharaoh has finally relented. We are all free to leave with our families and our possessions.

MIRIAM   That's fantastic!

AARON   But can we trust him? He's changed his mind so many times.

MOSES   That's true. His heart might be hardened again. That's why we have to leave as quickly as we can.

MIRIAM   But six hundred thousand people can't just jump up and leave. There are preparations to be made. What about food? If we don't bake, we'll starve out there.

MOSES   Good point. Still, we don't have time for any fancy braided hallah with brushed egg wash.

[Melody: "Surrey with the Fringe on Top" from *Oklahoma!*]

MOSES   *Moms and dads and kids better scurry,*
                 Grab some clothes and scram in a hurry,
                 Grab some clothes and scram in a hurry,
                 And you don't dare stop.

                 There's just time to flee our attacker,
                 There's no time to be a slow packer,
                 Or bake bread – well maybe a cracker
                 With some holes on top.

                 They're dry and tasteless,
                 They don't appetize,
                 There's not much here to redeem these.
                 But if you're clever, you can improvise
                 You'll find you enjoy them with cream cheese.

                 Sheets and sheets we'll eat as we run out,
                 Through the night, and then with the sun out.
                 Sheets and sheets we'll eat till we run out

In a week or so
When this holiday is over,
We can raise our dough!

***

MIRIAM   We've crossed the Red Sea!   Pharaoh's army is drowned!

AARON   Our people are safe at last.

MOSES   True, we don't have to worry about the Egyptians anymore. But I think there could still be hard times ahead. I'm already hearing the Israelites grumbling about what we may encounter in the wilderness.

MIRIAM   We can worry about that tomorrow. Today, it's all about celebrating. We're a free people – and one day we'll be a light to the nations. Right now I think my little brother deserves a big thank-you! Everybody – sing!

[Melody: "Mame" from *Mame*]

CHORUS   *You softened Pharaoh's heart for us all, Mo-ses.*
You gave us strength to answer the call, Mo-ses.
You may be slow of speech but your brother spins a tale
    to beat the band.
It's you we'll stand behind as you lead our people to the
    Promised Land.

You let us drop our mortar and bricks, Mo-ses,
With your ten plagues and various tricks, Mo-ses.
Whoever thought that someone found floating in the
    Nile would steal the show?
You've given us the prize again,
We said our quick good-byes again,
Someday our bread will rise again, Mo!

You made the waters part with your hand, Mo-ses,

So we could walk across on dry land, Mo-ses.
When we were safely through we all stood together and
         we watched with pride
The end of Pharaoh's army.
We're grateful that we've got you on our side.

We'll wander through the desert with you, Mo-ses.
Obey a stone commandment or two, Mo-ses.
Though we may tire of manna for breakfast, lunch, and
         dinner as we go,
We'll always be your children and,
We'll always lend a helping hand,
As we keep slogging through the sand –
Mo-o! Mo-o! Mo!!

From Regeneration to Regeneration

— a Doctor Who play —

The Doctor is an Elijah figure. It's inescapable. Unfettered by time, equipped with astonishing powers and irrepressible moral strength, both of these benevolent spirits travel through the ages defending the weak and supporting the cause of justice. In ever-changing forms, yet.

I'm not accusing the Doctor's creators of any sort of *copying*, you know; the series is highly original. There's just something we Jews have always loved about a time-traveling guest; we're always inviting Elijah to our seder, not to mention our babies' covenant ceremonies. We like the guy. We're used to him. And we welcome the Doctor, whatever number he may be, to take his place alongside our own Time Lord.

Uncle Yordi Merkava (the *yordei merkava* are the Jewish mystics who meditate upon Elijah's chariot), Aaron, and Mom/Elisheva are minor roles; the others have lots to say. Be aware that Aaron and Mom/Elisheva are a romantic interest.

THE PROPHET (ELIJAH)
HANNAH
YORDI (MERKAVA)
MOSES
AARON
MOM / ELISHEVA

MOM	Would you take these bowls to the table, Hannah, and make sure your brother's put the pillows on the chairs.
HANNAH	Okay. Where am I sitting, Mom?
MOM	Between Isaac and Uncle Yordi.
HANNAH	Do I have to let Isaac find the afikomen? Isn't he big enough for a fair contest now?
MOM	All right, you find it if you can. But you should let him open the door for Elijah.
HANNAH	That's all right. I'm tired of opening the door for nobody. Mainly I like all the singing. Hey, Uncle Yordi's here!
MOM	Hi, Yordi – happy Passover.
UNCLE YORDI	Hi, Lizzie. Gosh, that smells good. How am I going to last through two hours of seder before we eat?
HANNAH	You *always* say that, Uncle Yordi. Anyhow, you're sitting next to me, so you can show me all that crazy stuff in the haggadah.
UNCLE YORDI	Child, you wound me. There's nothing more serious than the haggadah. And I heard you say you open the door for nobody. You meant to say that you never see the prophet Elijah when you open the door?

HANNAH   Yes. It's silly.

UNCLE YORDI   You should be grateful you don't see the Prophet, Hannah. If you see him, one thing's for certain – we're all in danger.

HANNAH   Uncle Yordi! Elijah is supposed to announce the Messiah.

UNCLE YORDI   That will be his *last* appearance. Until then, he's a very, very busy prophet. Who knows how many disasters he's averted? If he's making house calls, then God help you.

HANNAH   Uncle, I love you but you do sometimes sound like a nutter. How do you know Elijah averts disasters? I didn't learn anything like that in Hebrew school. The Prophet gets invited to seders and brit milahs, and then tells everybody the Messiah's coming.

UNCLE YORDI   Look, I happen to have some news clippings ...

HANNAH   Of *course* you do.

UNCLE YORDI   Just have a look.   Here's a very well-known picture. Ever seen it?

HANNAH   Sure, that's the American sailor kissing a nurse in Times Square. The day Japan surrendered in 1945.

UNCLE YORDI   Except that's not a sailor. Look at that man on the left, a few feet back from the couple. If that nurse was not preoccupied with that surprising kiss, she would have seen that other man, begun talking with him, eventually falling in love and marrying him. A year later, they would have had a son.

HANNAH   So what's wrong with that?

UNCLE YORDI   You don't want to know.

HANNAH   Then who was the sailor?

UNCLE YORDI   That's what I'm *telling* you. He's the Prophet Elijah.

HANNAH   Uncle! Even if that's true – how would *you* know about it?

UNCLE YORDI   Not important. Anyway, it's classified. Now, look at this famous picture of construction workers eating lunch on a steel beam …

MOM   We're ready to begin. Everybody come to the table.

UNCLE YORDI   We'll talk later.

***

MOM   "In every generation there have been those who wished to destroy us, but the Holy One rescues us from their hands." Now, everybody, take your wineglass and pour a little into Elijah's cup. It will take all our efforts to bring the world's redemption.

    (The family beagle, Bagel, begins to yip and wag his tail.)

MOM   What's got into that dog? Hannah, would you please open the door for Elijah? I know you wanted Isaac to do it, but if he doesn't finish his soup it'll get cold. And let the dog out.

HANNAH   Oh, all right. *(Going to the door.)* Oh, who are *you* then?

THE PROPHET   I'm the Prophet. What's *your* name?

HANNAH   Um – Hannah. What … did you say you're …

THE PROPHET   Just so. Glad to meet you, Hannah. You wouldn't happen to have a mirror inside, would you? Yes, there's one! Excuse me. Ah, could have been worse. Look at the beard.

HANNAH   The Prophet? The Prophet Elijah?

THE PROPHET   Yes. I was invited, wasn't I? What a lovely seder table. Oh, there he is! I remember what a beautiful baby he was.

HANNAH   Who? My brother? Or Uncle Yordi? Or my grandfather?

THE PROPHET   Actually – all of them.

HANNAH   You really expect me to believe you're the Prophet Elijah? I happen to know that he lived thousands of years ago. While King Ahab was alive, and Jezebel.

THE PROPHET   Hannah, I am very, very impressed. I rarely meet children who pay attention in Hebrew school. You're quite right, I knew Ahab and Jezebel. They were repulsive, in case you're interested. Terrible table manners.

HANNAH   But … that would make you rather too old to, you know, be alive.

THE PROPHET   Hannah, don't let that trouble you one instant. I'm a time lord, actually. Mine isn't a typical life-span. Not really linear.

HANNAH   You're off your trolley. A lifetime is a lifetime. It has a beginning and an end.

THE PROPHET   Well, in terms of mortal consciousness, that appears to be true. But time isn't really like a line. It's more like a ball of wibbly-wobbly, timey-wimey – stuff. But, listen, Hannah, talking of time, I haven't much of it right now. I just dropped by for a bit of DNA. Specifically, your dad's. Or your brother's.

HANNAH   Some DNA? Are you planning to replicate them somewhere?

THE PROPHET   Dear, dear, you *do* have some outlandish ideas,

Hannah. No, I merely wish to use some Cohen Y chromosomes to steer myself back to the original Cohen, with whom I have some business.

HANNAH   You mean, to go back in time.

THE PROPHET   Yes indeed.

HANNAH   You can use *my* DNA.

THE PROPHET   Hannah, you are an extraordinarily intelligent young person, and brave as blazes, but I'm afraid you don't possess the Cohen Modal haplotype. It's only on the Y chromosome. And you're a girl.

HANNAH   Prophet, I'm not going back in there and telling my family that Elijah's in the vestibule waiting for a DNA sample.

THE PROPHET   I see your point. All right then, if you'll just nip upstairs to the lav and borrow your brother's hair-brush. I'll meet you outside.

HANNAH   All right then.

THE PROPHET   Smashing.

                              ***

THE PROPHET   Here you are! Good girl, you've got the brush. That'll do. I hope Isaac won't need it in the next few microseconds.

HANNAH   Look! What's that by the pavement? It's on fire! It's a bush!

THE PROPHET   Well …

HANNAH   Is that the burning bush?! The original burning bush?

THE PROPHET   Uh, it's – well, yes and no.

HANNAH   Is it, or isn't it?

THE PROPHET It's a vehicle for time travel. However, as far as Moses is concerned, it's a burning bush. That's how it's described in Exodus.

HANNAH I can't believe it! The burning bush! Shouldn't we take our shoes off then?

THE PROPHET Your socks would get dirty. Anyhow, I'm going to be getting into it in a moment, and I prefer to travel shod.

HANNAH You're getting into it?

THE PROPHET Yes. As I mentioned, it's a time-travel vehicle. It's more formally known as a Torah-Activated Relocation Device Imitating Shrubbery. It's about to take me back thirty-three centuries, for a very important meeting. Care to come along?

HANNAH You want me to go into a bush that's on fire?

THE PROPHET Forgive me. My previous transport was a fiery chariot. I always forget that others aren't as comfortable traveling in flames as I. That's why I usually come down your chimney to visit your seder!

HANNAH Wait – that's –

THE PROPHET No worries, Hannah, I will dial down the inferno to a comfortable twenty-four degrees Centigrade. So, are you in?

HANNAH If I don't go back to the table, I think my parents would panic.

THE PROPHET Your consideration is touching. However, they will never know about it, as you'll be returning here eight seconds after you went to open the door.

HANNAH Well – okay, then! Let's go!

THE PROPHET Brilliant! Now, just step through here – that's it – what do you think of my wheels, eh?

HANNAH   It's lovely. Seems like the inside is much bigger than the outside.

THE PROPHET   True. Right, then, let's scan your brother's priestly hair, and once it's digitalized – there – we send the Y-DNA sequence over to that scroll.

HANNAH   You know, that scroll looks just like a –

THE PROPHET   It is. If you'll just step over there and scroll down – there, use that wooden handle right there – scroll down till you see Exodus, six, twenty-three.

HANNAH   It's run out of battery.

THE PROPHET   Oh, did I forget to power off again? There, reach down and put that plug into the outlet. Not that one! Oh, bugger all.

                (There is a booming sound.)

HANNAH   What's happening?

THE PROPHET   We've just launched into the time vortex. Wonder where we're headed? What does the screen say?

HANNAH   It says Exodus, two, eleven.

THE PROPHET   We're definitely not headed for Aaron. We may meet his younger brother, though. Also one of your relatives.

HANNAH   Aaron's younger brother? But that's –

                (A crashing sound.)

THE PROPHET   Either we're in Thebes, or at a wrestling match. Think it's Thebes, though.

MOSES   Ugh! Awww … ow! Ow!

THE PROPHET   That fellow's getting the worst of it. But he didn't start this fight – that was the taskmaster. I suppose this is one good reason to have a sonic screwdriver

... bzzt! There. No more taskmaster.

MOSES   What happened? Where'd he go?

THE PROPHET The taskmaster?

MOSES   Yes. He was smiting a Hebrew slave. So I jumped him, but he got me into a head-lock.

THE PROPHET You're quite the martial artist, Moses. You struck him down and hid his body in the sand.

MOSES   Did I?

THE PROPHET Yes. You were simply pukka. Now, what you'd better do is skive off, since the Egyptian authorities will not be best pleased.

MOSES   But – I don't know where to go. I live here. I've never been anywhere else.

THE PROPHET Ah. Well, then, in you go. We'll give you a lift to Midian, because there'll be no end of trouble if you end up detained at Her Majesty's pleasure. *His* Majesty, I should say. Come on.

MOSES   This looks very much like a bush that's burning but not being consumed.

THE PROPHET It is. Get in anyway.

MOSES   I feel I should take the sandals off my feet.

THE PROPHET Don't let me stop you.

HANNAH   Are you actually Moses?

MOSES   That's what they call me, for short.

HANNAH   For short? What's your full name then?

MOSES   The same as my grandfather – Ramses Kanakht Khaemwaset – or something like that.

THE PROPHET   I'm sure there's a proper way to tell you this, but I don't know what it is, and at any rate, we haven't the time.   Moses, that wasn't your grandfather. You were born a Hebrew slave, you were adopted, and we're on our way to see your brother Aaron.

MOSES   *(pause)* Okay.

THE PROPHET   Just to ramp it up a bit, the importance of your meeting up with Aaron and taking him back to Egypt cannot be overstated.

MOSES   All right then.

THE PROPHET   But first I have to introduce Aaron to a bird.

MOSES   Is there anywhere I can sit down?

THE PROPHET   Over here.

HANNAH   A *bird*, Prophet – you're sounding pottier than usual, you know.

THE PROPHET   I *beg* your pardon, Hannah, I meant a *girl*.   Aaron is in danger of missing a rather important chat with a girl named Elisheva. He's a bit bashful and needs some encouragement, that's all.

HANNAH   And if he misses this chat, then what?

THE PROPHET   Then he won't see what a terrific bird she is, he won't fall in love with her, and that means, dearest Hannah, there won't ever be any Cohens. Because he's the first. He may be painfully shy, but history cannot allow him to remain a bachelor.

HANNAH   Then we'd better get moving, hadn't we?

THE PROPHET   Off we go then, just a short hop – Exodus six, I think it was. Just pull down that handle … here it is, job done. Look there, it's Aaron.

MOSES   That's my brother?

THE PROPHET   You can't miss the resemblance.

AARON   Moses? Is it really you?

THE PROPHET   It's he. Moses, this is your older brother Aaron. You were both born into a family of Levites, which are the priests of Israel, and Aaron here is going to be the High Priest, the Kohen Gadol. As will his *progeny* be, also.

AARON   I haven't any progeny.

THE PROPHET   Yes, I know. Aaron, I'd like you to come with me over to that well.

AARON   But I'm not thirsty.

THE PROPHET   Doesn't matter. Oh! Bring that goat with you. It looks *extremely* thirsty.

AARON   What? Should I – should I pick it up, or what?

HANNAH   Here, it has a leash. Take the leash, Aaron, and walk over to the well.

AARON   There's a lot of girls over there. No, really, I can't. I don't want to.

MOSES   Aaron. Do it.

ELISHEVA   Oooh, look at that little *goat!* It's so *cute!* Can I pet him?

AARON   *(pause)* Uh, sure. Sure, go ahead.

ELISHEVA   Here's a drink, goaty. What's his name?

THE PROPHET   *(whispers)* Chad!

AARON   Chad. It's, it's, his name is Chad.

MOSES   And I thought *I* was slow of speech.

THE PROPHET   Don't worry, it's temporary.

ELISHEVA   Chad's adorable. My family would just *love* him!
              Do you think you could bring him over sometime?

AARON   Uh ...

HANNAH   *(whispers)* Sure!

AARON   Sure! Um ... where do you live?

THE PROPHET   *(whispers)* Good, that's very good.

ELISHEVA   That big tent, over there. With the camel in front.
              When do you think you can come over?

THE PROPHET   *(whispers)* In a very, very short time.

AARON   Really soon.

ELISHEVA   Fantastic! I hope you can stay for dinner. Ta!

MOSES   Better not give back that goat, Aaron. Offer to buy
              it.

AARON   Well, how much should I offer?

MOSES   No more than two zuzim. Any more is a rip-off.

THE PROPHET   Excellent. Aaron, mind you show up to her place
              for dinner. She's cute, isn't she?

AARON   She's really very pretty.

THE PROPHET   I think you'll also find she's wise, strong, compas-
              sionate, and loyal.

HANNAH   You're pretty good at this, Prophet. Do you match
              up people a lot?

THE PROPHET   Once in a while. Usually I visit poor people dis-
              guised as a beggar.

HANNAH   The point of that being?

THE PROPHET   Oh, I find out if they're goodhearted, and then if
              they are, I let them know there's a treasure in their

wall, or some such. More often, I avert disaster.

HANNAH   In between all those seders and brisses?

THE PROPHET Yes. I move around a lot. It keeps me young.

HANNAH   I imagine people start to recognize you, after a while.

THE PROPHET Actually, no. I look different every time I appear.

HANNAH   How does that work?

THE PROPHET Sometimes it's a simple disguise, and other times I'm a completely different person. When I get old, I re-generate.

HANNAH   What? You just grow a new body, then?

THE PROPHET Yes, it's rather convenient, too. Hate to see what my original incarnation would look like after 2900 years. So! We're nearly done here. We should send Moses and Aaron back to Egypt adequately prepared, though.

MOSES   Prepared for what?

THE PROPHET Well, as you know, Moses, or will know soon, you are to convince the Pharaoh to free all the Hebrew slaves. Pharaoh is *not* so inclined, however. You will have to be awfully persuasive.

MOSES   But I'm *not* particularly persuasive. I don't really think Aaron is, either.

THE PROPHET Right.   So this is what we'll do. Hand me that shepherd's staff, please, Moses.

MOSES   Here you go.

THE PROPHET Let's see, now – there should be a battery cover or something – yes, here it is. Now, look, here's a compartment in this staff. *Just* the right size for –

this.

AARON   What the blazes is *that?*

THE PROPHET   It's a sonic screwdriver. Very handy. Does lots of things. You'll need it if you have to remote-control other devices, such as someone else's staff. It also can track, and summon, alien life forms, such as blood-breathing frogs and hail-eating locusts. Just imagine how impressive you'll be with this in your hand! Can't begin to tell you how convenient mine's been.

MOSES   So you're telling me this is all I need to free the Hebrew slaves?

THE PROPHET   Afraid not. You'll actually need some outside help. That's where it gets dicey. The Pharaoh isn't going to fold till he faces the lonely assassin.

AARON   I'm already terrified.

THE PROPHET   You should be. It's the Weeping Angel – the most dangerous psychopath that ever existed.

HANNAH   I don't think we should be joining forces with psychopaths!

THE PROPHET   I'm not saying I *like* it. I'm saying it's the only thing that can break the Pharaoh. The Weeping Angel feeds on time energy; it sends its victims into the past, and absorbs the energy left behind. Really diabolical, although you must admit it's not the worst way to go.

HANNAH   Now, Prophet, how will this work, without us becoming its victims?

THE PROPHET   That's the brilliant part! The Angel can't move while it's being observed. It can only move about in the dark when no one can see it. Now, one way to control it is to look at it without blinking. Just try doing that for awhile, it's bloody difficult. But I have something right here that watches and never blinks. Look.

HANNAH   It's a little blue eye. Looks like glass.

AARON   I've seen those. It's called a nazar. You hang it around your neck, or over a baby's crib. It turns away the demons.

THE PROPHET   It turns away the *Weeping Angel*. Good thing, too – otherwise the past would be crowded with confused time-wanderers. Come to think of it, it already is.

MOSES   Okay, so we hang a nazar on all the slaves' houses. Then what?

THE PROPHET   The Egyptian custom is that the first-born of a household answers the door when someone knocks. Let loose the Angel – before you know it, those firstborn are swept back to whatever century and the Angel's chowing down on their energy. The Pharaoh freaks out, the slaves are freed, and Bob's your uncle.

HANNAH   Prophet, are you sure you want to put Moses and Aaron in such terrible danger? Moses and Aaron, of all people?

THE PROPHET   No danger at all, Hannah. I quite assure you – I've looked at this story from every possible angle, including hindsight, and your ancestors are perfectly safe wearing the nazar. Here you go, friends, hang these round your necks.

MOSES   Well, thank you, Elijah, you've been most kind.

AARON   I suppose we're ready for Egypt, then.

THE PROPHET   It's my pleasure. Can't wait to read all about it.

HANNAH   Aaron, congratulations. On meeting Elisheva, and all.

AARON	Thank you. I hope that works out all right.
HANNAH	I'm pretty sure it will.
AARON	I'm not sure I caught your name?
HANNAH	I'm Hannah Cohen.
AARON	Hannah – Cohen. Ah. And, from what century?
HANNAH	The twenty-first. C.E.
AARON	Just so. I guess I'd best go meet Elisheva's parents.
HANNAH	I think so too.
MOSES	And thanks for the lift, Prophet. Very impressive vehicle, that. I doubt I'll ever forget it.
THE PROPHET	And I think we'd better get in it. Do I hear – Hannah, do you hear that? I think someone's calling my name.
MOM	*(sings)* Eliahu ha-navee, Eliahu ha-tishbi …
HANNAH	It's my mom. At the seder.
AARON	What a sweet voice.
THE PROPHET	It is. Hannah, we need to get you home.
MOSES	Shalom, friends. Thanks for all the help.
THE PROPHET	Look. We're arriving.
HANNAH	This is amazing. It took no time at all.
THE PROPHET	Wibbly-wobbly, you know.
HANNAH	I think that's my driveway. Prophet, where will you go now? Will you be all right?
THE PROPHET	Hannah, I won't go far.
HANNAH	Will I see you again?

THE PROPHET   You will. But you might not know it.

HANNAH   You're wonderful. I'm going back inside now.

THE PROPHET   Keep singing for me, Hannah.

UNCLE YORDI   We'll all sing for you, Prophet. The universe will sing for you. The song is ending, but the story never ends.

Ten Plagues, You're Out!

— a baseball play-by-play —

As has been pointed out in many a documentary and book, baseball was an important cultural point of entry for the Jews who immigrated to America from 1883 to 1920, and their children. Feeling very alien in the golden land of their dreams, they embraced this most prominent passion of Americans. These and other immigrants soon saw that baseball is, not the civil religion of America, but its language. The game channels strong emotions, forms communities, and provides a line of communication between people who otherwise have nothing to say to each other – most notably, family members. It is one of the nation's greatest treasures. For millions of Jews, it was our American membership card.

Those lofty thoughts having been expressed, this *shpiel* is a shameless and silly vehicle for puns. It's also a sort of puzzle that challenges you to find the Exodus and seder references during the broadcast.

The two major characters are Nix Levin (play-by-play) and Diane Noo (color commentary). The Voiceover has six commercials and such to read, and Aaron HaKohen and Moe Ziss both get interviewed. Beth Shalom and Abraham Avinu have brief appearances.

NIX LEVIN
DIANE NOO
MOE ZISS
VOICEOVER
AARON (HAKOHEN)
BETH SHALOM
ABRAHAM (AVINU)

NIX LEVIN   Welcome to Burning Bush Stadium in Luxor,
                   Egypt, and today's broadcast of what promises to
                   be a classic matchup. The Nile Egyptians are host-
                   ing their division rivals, the Goshen Hebrews, and
                   there's a lot riding on this game. I'd like to wel-
                   come my partner in the broadcast booth, Diane
                   Noo.

DIANE NOO   Why, thank you, Nix, and I couldn't agree more
                   about the importance of this game. With a win to-
                   night, the Goshen Hebrews can move on to face the
                   leader of the Sinai League, and the Hebrews could
                   sure use that shot of confidence for the road games
                   ahead.

NIX LEVIN   Starting today for the Egyptians is veteran right-
                   hander Fay Row, who is twelve and four this sea-
                   son, and he's coming off a solid performance
                   against the Hittites last week. On the mound for
                   Goshen is Moe Ziss, a rookie lefthander just up
                   from triple-A and, my, what he must be feeling
                   right about now!

DIANE NOO   You're not kidding, Nix, and here's what Moe had
                   to say a little earlier about facing the impressive
                   Nile lineup.

                   Moe, what's on your mind when you're preparing
                   to face last year's division champions?

MOE ZISS   Well, it's, it's like a mental game, you have to be
                   willing to throw on the corners even when you're

behind in the c-c-count. You just, just need the confidence to do that.

DIANE NOO   What about the breaking ball, Moe? Your manager Aaron HaKohen says it's the your most valuable pitch. How do you plan to use that?

MOE ZISS   What I want to do is make the b-b-batters commit early. If I can get hitters to l-l-look for my pitch, they'll swing at outside p-p-pitches.

DIANE NOO   Hey, good luck tonight on the hill, Moe.

MOE ZISS   Thanks, Diane.

NIX LEVIN   He's a talented pitcher, and we wish him the best tonight as he takes on the Egyptians in his first major league start.

DIANE NOO   He might have been a little nervous earlier today, but the Hebrews' scout saw something special in him, and that's why he's here this evening.

NIX LEVIN   And we'll be back with the first pitch after this message.

VOICEOVER   What do I want? I want horsepower. Cleaner horsepower. I want power that dominates the desert, and I want to go the distance without frequent fill-ups. Give me the rush of 200 horsepower. I want the best of both worlds. Introducing the all-new Camel Hybrid. From Toyota.

NIX LEVIN   Welcome back to Burning Bush Stadium, as the Canaanite Sports Network brings you tonight's broadcast of the deciding game of the Dynastic League series between the Nile Egyptians and the Goshen Hebrews. The managers have exchanged their lineup cards, and the Egyptians have taken the field. Fay Row on the mound. Batting first for the Hebrews is Manny Shtanna. It's a fastball – swing and a miss. Nothing and one on Shtanna.

The out-of-town crowd is here in force, and you can hear them chanting his name.

DIANE NOO   You know, Nix, this team is known for taking a lot of pitches, and that's going to be the problem for Row – the patient hitters on this Hebrews team are too numerous for him, and he's going to have to throw strikes to keep the bases clear when the big guys come up.

NIX LEVIN   Fay Row with the windup, it's the change-up and, whoops, it hits Shtanna. Manny Shtanna goes to first, and here comes Reed Basket, the big veteran, hitting righthanded. It's the curve, that Basket takes low. One and 0. Fay Row doesn't like the sign. Now he sees one he likes. Fastball pitch and it's a line drive to center. Deal Shrewdly charges, but it falls in front of him and Basket has a single. The Hebrews have men on first and second here at the top of the first, and nobody out.

DIANE NOO   Fay Row's looking a little desperate now as he's about to face the heart of the order. It won't be easy to shake off that pitch lined by Reed Basket.

NIX LEVIN   Here's first baseman Stretch Forth, batting third. Still nobody out. Looks like manager Curt Magician is trotting out for a talk with –

VOICEOVER   This is a test. For the next sixty seconds, this station will conduct a test of the Egyptian Floodcast System. This is only a test.

(A long beep.)

VOICEOVER   This has been a test of the Egyptian Floodcast System. If this had been an actual flood of the Nile River, you would have been instructed where to tune in your area for news and instructions.

DIANE NOO   … sure Hebrews fans are satisfied with the first inning. Hebrews lead two nothing, and let's have a look at the Fan Cam. We have some celebrities in attendance today. There's pop star Miriam Navia, enjoying an evening at the park with her friends. She's got her Hebrews jersey on. And just a few rows back is Manny Shtanna's fiancé, Lyla Hazeh. Lovely lady.

NIX LEVIN   Look, there they are – everybody's favorite family!

DIANE NOO   That's right, it's Pa Slee and Ma Ror. And their four sons. They all have popcorn and peanuts, but I see one of them who's not too happy to be here.

NIX LEVIN   We know he's not a big baseball fan. He's just here because he has to be.

DIANE NOO   Still, I'm not sure he should be dropping peanut shells down on the next level.

⋆⋆⋆

DIANE NOO   All right, we're at the bottom of the second inning at Burning Bush Stadium, two men out, and Moe Ziss is on the hill. He struck out three in the first, and let's see how he handles Egyptian left fielder Taz Master.

NIX LEVIN   Ziss winds up – releases – oh, Taz Master's hit by the pitch, and he's down. The trainer's rushing over to the plate. It looks serious for Taz. I'm not seeing any movement. They're waving for the cart … this doesn't look good at all.

DIANE NOO   Moe looks pretty worried too. He's known for his control and I don't recall anything like this happening with him before.

NIX LEVIN   With a pause in the action, let's hear a word from one of our sponsors.

VOICEOVER   Badder. Bolder. McMatza is revving up the dollar menu with our new hot 'n' spicy Chicken

McMatza. Baked with savory sauce and sizzling spices. All for just a dollar. Can you handle more to love for less? McMatza – it's not just fast food anymore. We love to see you smile!

***

NIX LEVIN   Glad you could join us here at Burning Bush Stadium tonight for this matchup of the Nile Egyptians and the Goshen Hebrews. Three innings complete, and the score is Hebrews two, Egyptians nothing. Goshen manager Aaron HaKohen is speaking with us from the dugout – Aaron, how are you feeling about your rookie pitcher right now?

AARON   Well, Nix, I couldn't be more pleased with this fellow, and we're sure glad to have him.

NIX LEVIN   I was about to say, this *young* rookie pitcher, but that's not really the case with Moe, is it?

AARON   *(laughing)* No, not really, Nix, you don't see that many eighty-year-old rookies. He's spent a good part of his career in the wilderness league, and we just feel lucky that he was ready for this change.

DIANE NOO   Aaron, there's been recent speculation that Major League Baseball is considering abolishing the reserve clause in favor of free agency. How would that affect your team?

AARON   Well, my view is that the reserve clause amounts to restraint of trade, and it takes away players' freedom to control their own careers. I know it benefits a team to reserve rights to a player, for a period of time after his contract expires, and maybe that's necessary to keep salaries from getting out of hand. But in the case of this league – gee. A four-hundred-year reserve clause seems a little over the top. I think it has to go, and I think my club, and all the clubs, just have to accept what comes. You can't confine players like that. You have to let them go.

NIX LEVIN   We'll let *you* go, Aaron. Thanks for your time.

AARON   Pleasure talking with you, Nix.

***

DIANE NOO   Top of the fifth inning, Hebrews have added to their lead, it's four to nothing over the Egyptians. Fay Row is back on the mound facing Hebrews shortstop Chad Gadya, who's just up from the farm system where he hit a solid .290 this season.

NIX LEVIN   Chad was acquired at the end of last season, and the Hebrews picked him up fairly cheap. He has a two-year, two-zuzim contract. Quite a talented fielder. Here's the windup. Gadya swings – and misses. That one was nowhere near the strike zone, what was he thinking?

DIANE NOO   Sort of looked like a curve, sort of didn't.

NIX LEVIN   Row's not waiting for a sign – he winds up, and here comes another odd pitch. Swing and a miss. Don't think I've ever seen a curve like that. 0 and two.

DIANE NOO   Chad's pointing at the catcher's mitt. He wants the ump to have a look at the ball. Let's see if we can zoom in on this – yes, I think there's something strange about that baseball. It's got a dark patch on it.

NIX LEVIN   Red, I think. Diane, that could be blood.

DIANE NOO   Could be. You know, Nix, baseball's been plagued by this kind of misbehavior on the part of pitchers for quite a while now, and I wouldn't be surprised if the Commissioner gets involved. Fay Row will be lucky if he gets to stay in this game. Looks like he's just getting a warning, though.

NIX LEVIN   Here's the 0-two pitch. Grounder to third. Glass up with it, he throws to first, and it's one out. That brings up Lando Goshen, great name for the Hebrews' right fielder, and the outfield is moving in.

DIANE NOO   It was raining earlier today, and the grass near the right-field warning track is slick. You can actually see some puddling. This has been a problem with Burning Bush Stadium for eons. I was talking to an old timer recently who said they used to call it the 'Frog Bog,' and it was really a hazard for outfielders chasing a fly.

NIX LEVIN   Let's hope the Frog Bog doesn't take a toll on our teams today.   Here's the windup – swing and a miss. It's 0 and one. Lando's been stymied lately by the slider.

DIANE NOO   He's still a good hitter, Nix, and I'm not sure but the Egyptian outfielders are making a mistake moving in. Lando is a smart hitter.

NIX LEVIN   Here's the pitch – and Goshen connects for a towering fly ball into right field! Back goes Deal Shrewdly, it's headed toward the wall, don't think he can make it – oh, he slipped and can't get it. Lando Goshen's headed for second. Breddo Affliction gets there to scoop it up, but his throw to third is not in time, and Lando Goshen has a triple. One out, and a man on third.

DIANE NOO   That'll be scored an error on Deal Shrewdly. Looks like the Frog Bog's claimed a victim, here in the fourth.

NIX LEVIN   Coming to the plate is Rod Smite, the Big Jewnit. How'd he ever get a moniker like that, Diane?

DIANE NOO   His dad likes to tell the story about when Rod was in Little League, he had a case of head lice and they wouldn't let him use his locker. Kind of embarrassing, really. But, you know, it's almost a rite of passage with most kids, everybody gets them one time or another.

NIX LEVIN   That may be why Rod keeps his head shaved.

DIANE NOO   Could be. I could understand that. Lice are a real pestilence.

NIX LEVIN   Smite watches strike one go by. Fay Row eyes the man on third. Unwinds, and Rod lines it to short. The shortstop snags it and throws to third. Goshen tries to dive back but it's a double play to end the inning.

DIANE NOO   It's still four-nothing Hebrews. We'll move on to the bottom of the fifth right after this.

VOICEOVER   Pithom Depot is more than a store. It's a store city. Whether it's supplies, tools, or just a little advice, we've got you covered. Come to Pithom Depot and get started on that 'to-do' list. This week, save fifty percent on twenty-pound bags of Thutmose straw-and-mud mix. Only at Pithom Depot. You can do it. We can help.

NIX LEVIN   Moe Ziss is on the mound facing the Nile Egyptians' second baseman Rocky Hart. Hart has had some problems with consistency this season – you never know what you'll get when he comes to the plate. He's streaky. Moe Ziss throws, and it's outside. Moe pauses a moment, throws again – it's a fastball and Hart hits it to right. Reed Basket can't reach it in time, and Hart has a single.

DIANE NOO   At the plate now is Wayne Glass. It seems to me, Nix, that without a lot of power in the Nile lineup, they're relying on strategy to move the runners forward.

NIX LEVIN   Ziss with his windup – it's a changeup, but Glass connects and it's a high fly – Lando Goshen's under it and makes the catch.

DIANE NOO   Now Motsa Bry is up, and after him Bit Herb, and either of those are a threat. So Alfy Komen's walking over to the mound to confer with his pitcher.

NIX LEVIN   Ziss glances at Hart on first. Throws, and Bry hits a high fly ball to left – Basket under it, and two away.

DIANE NOO   Moe has got to control this swarm of fly balls. Maybe he'll try the curve. Rocky Hart isn't the fastest runner, though, and he's taking a big lead off the bag. Might just be his way of throwing off the pitcher.

NIX LEVIN   Here comes Bit Herb to the plate.

DIANE NOO   By the way, this is his nine-hundred and fifty-second game in his six years with the Egyptians. He hasn't missed a single game, and that's a record in this league.

NIX LEVIN   That's why they call him the Iron Horse.

DIANE NOO   His teammates have changed that name recently, Nix. Bit Herb's been on a hitting streak for nearly four weeks now, and he's superstitious. Hasn't changed his socks in all that time. So they're calling him the Iron Horseradish.

NIX LEVIN   Glad it's not me doing the locker-room interviews.

DIANE NOO   His teammates wouldn't mind seeing the end of that streak.

NIX LEVIN   Herb takes one low and outside. There are two outs and a man on first. Ziss into his windup and the one-0 pitch is a slider. Herb hits another high one to left, and Reed Basket's under it. Side retired. At the end of five, it's Hebrews four, Egyptians nothing. We'll be back in a moment.

VOICEOVER I know how much my cattle love me. From the moment they jump into bed to wake me up every morning, to the tail-wagging hello I get when I come home and open the door. They're my best friends. I'd do anything to keep them happy and healthy. That's why I buy Scarab Guard. It's the one cattle medicine that's guaranteed to keep away disease-causing scarabs for up to a month. Scarab Guard. When you want the best, for your best friends.

NIX LEVIN Back at the park now, as Nile manager Curt Magician has a look at Fay Row's pitching hand. I think he has a blister or a boil on the base of his thumb, there.

DIANE NOO Wouldn't surprise me at all, Nix, with the sort of shenanigans we've seen from Row earlier in the game, like those bloodballs he *may* have been throwing in the fourth inning. Sort of a cosmic justice going on, if that's the case.

NIX LEVIN Row doesn't want to come out of the game, though if I'm reading the body language right, his manager has some doubts. Magician's going back to the dugout. Looks like Row's staying in the game.

DIANE NOO While Curt was looking at Row's finger, everyone else was looking up at the sky, which has clouded over quickly in the last few minutes. The forecast didn't call for rain or even clouds, so this is unexpected.

(Popping sounds.)

NIX LEVIN How about that!

DIANE NOO We've got a hailstorm going on here.

NIX LEVIN The players and the umps are taking cover in the dugouts, and the fans are streaming toward the concessions. The tarps are coming out, and we're in a weather delay.

DIANE NOO   Well, we're in the sixth inning, so it's an official game. Let's wait and see how long this lasts, and what the officials decide to do.

VOICEOVER   Drawn from the pure crystal waters of the Nile Delta, refreshing Rolling Ra Beer is the perfect ending to a summer day on the cataracts. Twenty generations of Egyptian master brewers have crafted the finest refreshment a man can drink. Free Flowing Rolling Ra. Good things come to those who wait.

NIX LEVIN   We're back at Burning Bush Stadium, and the weather delay is over as quickly as it started. The tarps are rolled back, it's the top of the sixth, and Fay Row is back on the mound with two out. The fans are getting cranky – Nile fans because their team is four runs down to a team they don't consider much of a challenge, and Goshen fans because they don't care for Fay Row's antics.

DIANE NOO   That shrill clacking sound you hear is baseball's newest heir to the thunder-stick and the homer hankie. Hebrews fans are afflicting Fay Row with locusts. I don't know how they got into the stadium –

NIX LEVIN   I think there are vendors outside.

DIANE NOO   – but those bugs make quite a racket. If the Hebrews fans are trying to rattle the pitcher, it's working. He's walked three in a row, the bases are loaded, all with two outs. Here comes Alfy Komen. All season, Alfy's given Row trouble, and he's threatening to put this game out of reach.

NIX LEAVEN   The pitch, swung on, up the middle, through the hole into left center field! Chad Gadya comes home, Lando Goshen's being waved around and Rod Smite is trying for third. Here's the throw, and they got him. He's tagged out, and the side is re-tired, but not before Alfy Komen crumbles the Egyptian defense and it's a six-nothing game through five and a half.

***

DIANE NOO   Our colleague Beth Shalom is in the stands with one of our favorite old-timers, Abraham Avinu. He was catcher with the original Canaan Hebrews before the team moved to Goshen. Down to you, Beth.

BETH SHALOM   Abraham, it's great to see you.

ABRAHAM   Great to be here, Beth. Great game.

BETH SHALOM   What do you think of this rookie's first start, Abra-ham?

ABRAHAM   I like what I see. Great pitching requires a certain amount of courage, as well as consistency. If a pitch isn't working, you have to be willing to move to another place. And you have to throw a lot of strikes, get the batters swinging. Of course, occa-sionally it's gonna cost you. You have to be willing to make a sacrifice sometimes.

BETH SHALOM   What do you think of Moe Ziss?

ABRAHAM   I think he's going to take this team great places, Beth – oh!

BETH SHALOM   My goodness! The stadium lights just went out.

DIANE NOO   For our radio audience – we're in darkness at Burn-ing Bush Stadium.

NIX LEVIN   I wonder if it has something to do with the con-struction going on in the Luxor high-rises next door.

DIANE NOO   Well, the power's not out since the microphones are still working … it's just the lights.

NIX LEVIN   Then it must be a breaker in the engineering room.

DIANE NOO   It's pretty dark in here, Nix; you can't see your hand in front of your face. If the fans try to leave, it could be dangerous.

NIX LEVIN   I just noticed that there's still light on in the Hebrews dugout.

DIANE NOO   Possibly they have a generator. I think that's Curt Magician coming over to confer with Aaron HaKohen. This is a scary situation. Beth, if you can hear me, can you get over to the visitors' dugout and see what you can find out?

BETH SHALOM   I've managed to get over here, and as I'm listening it seems that Magician is asking HaKohen to turn the lights back on. I'm not sure why he thinks Aaron has the capacity to do that.

NIX LEVIN   Aaron majored in electrical engineering in college, but I wouldn't think – hey, there, the lights are back on. What a relief! The fans are cheering.

DIANE NOO   This is turning out to be one unforgettable baseball game.

NIX LEVIN   Let's hope we can get through the last two innings without further incident. Everyone's nerves are shaken.

DIANE NOO   The crew chief is waving the players back onto the field. Moe Ziss comes to the mound, tosses a few warmup pitches. I've noticed that one of the Hebrew fans in attendance has been keeping track of Moe's strikeouts faithfully by painting a red K for each one on the top of the visitors' dugout. And with the performance of this phenom tonight, the lintels are now covered in red.

NIX LEVIN   Egyptians first baseman Bunch Hyssop is at the

plate, batting right-handed. Moe waits for his sign. Unwinds, and it's a fastball. Bunch pops up and it's an easy out. That was a 95-mile-an-hour heater. Moe doesn't show any sign of fatigue. He may go the distance.

DIANE NOO   He pitched a lot of complete games in the minor leagues. This guy is known for endurance. He throws a lot of strikes, as Abraham pointed out, and keeps his pitch count low. Very smart player.

NIX LEVIN   Batting ninth is the pitcher, Fay Row, facing Moe Ziss. I am really surprised, Diane, that the Egyptians haven't sent up a pinch-hitter. I see activity in the bullpen. Moe is a very even-tempered pitcher, but there's some history between these two teams, and a somewhat tense atmosphere. Even a rookie pitcher knows he has to protect his players.

DIANE NOO   Since Fay Row has little chance of getting to base, I think Moe –

NIX LEVIN   No, Row is hit by a fastball! The Egyptians flood out of the dugout. This doesn't look good.

DIANE NOO   I'm not sure where he was hit.

NIX LEVIN   Where it hurts, Diane. It looks like the Nile pitcher is headed for the clubhouse – he's done for tonight – and the umpire's called time. Nile manager Curt Magician sends in the speedy Alex Andria to run for Fay Row. The Goshen players are moving back to their positions, and the Egyptians to the dugout. Here comes Drew Attawater to the plate.

DIANE NOO   Attawater's had a very good season, getting to base nearly four times in every ten appearances. He can read pitchers quite well, and let's see how he handles Moe Ziss.

NIX LEVIN   Here's the pitch – and Attawater hits a slow roller toward second, Rod Smite's got it, steps on the bag and fires it to Forth, double play and the inning is over without any runs.

DIANE NOO   To start the ninth, Curt Magician's going to send in his recent acquisition from Japan. This young man is wearing the number 1 on his uniform, which is unusual for a pitcher here, but possibly not overseas.

NIX LEVIN   So, number one Miyo Daya takes the hill, and he's facing the Hebrews' second baseman Angelo Death. He's a very dangerous hitter with a .380 average, and Miyo Daya has his hands full with the bases loaded, two outs.

First pitch, it's high and outside. Death is waiting for a pitch he likes … the windup, and Daya throws a curveball. Angelo connects with a high fly ball to left … will it stay in play? Breddo Affliction is moving back, back to the wall, leaps – but it's over his head and into the stands.

DIANE NOO   Angelo Death has a grand slam home run, and Breddo Affliction has hit the left field wall, and he's down. Breddo Affliction isn't rising and his manager and trainer are heading to the outfield to see what's going on.

NIX LEVIN   The score is now ten-nothing. There's been an incredible amount of injuries in this game.

DIANE NOO   Yes, tonight's been a world of hurt.

NIX LEVIN   I'm sure both these teams are going to be glad to see the last out of this game. Affliction is up and he's okay. Manny Shtanna's at the plate, and Miyo Daya winds up for his pitch. It's a high pop along the first base line … Stretch Forth makes the catch, and the inning is over.

DIANE NOO   Not sure if he's going to be able to ease the tension around here, but Mummy the Nile mascot is dancing around in the lower level seats. Usually he's a pretty good distraction when the team's behind. But the fans are still restless tonight, and nobody's taking up his offer to unwrap his linen.

NIX LEVIN   He should stick to shooting T-shirts into the stands. This game is brought to you under broadcasting rights granted by Major League Baseball, solely for the private, non-commercial use of our audience. Any cuneiform, heiroglyphic or other inscriptions of the game without the express written consent of Major League Baseball is prohibited.

DIANE NOO   We're in the bottom of the ninth inning here at Burning Bush Stadium, and the Hebrews are leading the Egyptians ten-nothing. Moe Ziss, who started this game, is on the mound to finish it, and it's been a masterful performance by this rookie left-hander from Midian. Earlier, Moe talked with us about his specialty pitch, which we haven't seen yet tonight.

Moe, tell us about this interesting changeup you've been working on.

MOE ZISS   Well, I grip the top of the ball with my first two fingers, and you see the w-w-word Cairo, in red lettering, here between the seams?

DIANE NOO   Yes, the letter C is right in the middle of your grip.

MOE ZISS   I f-f-find this grip sends the ball spinning pretty hard and it's hard to tell where it's changing direction.

DIANE NOO   Got a name for this pitch?

MOE ZISS   I dunno … Since I grip it this way, I g-g-guess you could call it the red C splitter.

DIANE NOO   Good luck with that tonight, Moe.

MOE ZISS   Thanks, Diane.

NIX LEVIN   The Egyptians are down to their last two outs. Rocky Hart struck out, and Wayne Glass is at the plate hoping to start a late rally for the Egyptians. It's a curve ball and Glass swings, and misses. Ziss gets his sign, unleashes another curve, and Glass is fooled once again. It's 0 and two. Nobody on.

DIANE NOO   The Egyptian lineup is really struggling against this very resourceful rookie.

NIX LEVIN   Moe is rapidly becoming a favorite with his fans. I'm seeing a sign that says "Everything's Coming Up Moe Ziss." And there's another one: "Moe Jo." He winds up, and he's caught Glass with the red C splitter. Two men out, and the Egyptians have just one more chance to catch the Hebrews. Deal Shrewdly's at the plate. Ziss gets his signal, throws – fouled off to the right. 0 and one. The windup – and it's a strike, Shrewdly's caught looking. Nothing and two.

DIANE NOO   There's no Champagne in the Hebrews' locker room tonight; whatever happens, they're on the road right after the game, and leaving the celebrations for later.

NIX LEVIN   The pitch, the swing – and Moe Ziss ends the game with a wicked sinker ball. The Egyptians are sunk by the sinker. Put it in the book! The Goshen Hebrews defeat the Nile Egyptians ten to nothing, and advance to the Sinai series.

DIANE NOO   I've never seen a game like this before, Nix, and I don't mind saying I'll be telling my grandkids about it someday.

NIX LEVIN   No question about it, Diane, this game is history. The Hebrews, and particularly their newest addition Moe Ziss, are a force to be reckoned with.

This final game of the Dynastic League series has been brought to you by the Canaanite Sports Network. For my partner Diane Noo and myself, Nix Levin, we thank you for joining us, and hope we'll see you next year in Jerusalem.

Good night from Burning Bush Stadium.

Trial by Jewry

— a Gilbert & Sullivan operetta —

I think it was Dr. Sigmund Freud who started the conversation about the upside-down nature of the Moses hero-myth. A classical hero is generally high-born, often of royal blood, but because of violent pursuit by his father, he is raised by peasants, slaves, or animals. He returns to his father-figure, challenges him, and conquers him.

The Hebrew myth, in contrast, has a slave-born hero who is adopted into a royal family. After that, he has the usual hero biography, with the unique injection of ethically-grounded mandates and the Israelite details. The surprise is that our ancestors' primary prophet and teacher was of lowly origin.

This isn't the Bible's only case of a shocking reversal of a social norm. Primogeniture, for example, the ancient world's standard procedure of giving the eldest son the family's leadership, is violated again and again: by the elevation of Isaac, of Jacob, and of Joseph over their older brothers, through divine intervention.

Well, when you think of social reversals, you naturally think of Gilbert and Sullivan. That was their meat and potatoes. The G&S operettas romp through the chambers of dignified society, and the snooty always end up flat on their pretentious pants. I figured, why not give Pharaoh the treatment?

Like the plots of the Gilbert and Sullivan operettas, this plot won't stand up to very close scrutiny. If you want storytelling that's faithful to the original – well, if that's what you want, I have no idea why you're reading this book.

If you and your guests are extremely familiar with the G&S opus, then perhaps you won't need too much preparation. But if you don't know the songs absolutely cold, I would suggest a few run-throughs before the seder.

PHARAOH
MOSES
THE PLAGUES
VIZIER
AARON
(LITTLE) AMULET
CHORUS

AMULET   Hail, Hebrew slaves, embittered by privation! To
              see your pain and woe touches my pitying soul.
              Each day, from dawn to dusk, you toil to build the
              Egyptian store-cities of Pithom and Ramses.
              Whence may comfort come to you as you labor?

AARON   The only sweetness in our lives is our ancient tradi-
              tion, the inheritance of our ancestors. And of
              course, the occasional visits from your rosy, round,
              smiling self.

AMULET   Rosy, am I? Smiling, am I? But alas, my brick-
              making friend, hast thou ever thought that beneath
              my merry exterior there may lurk a canker-worm
              of sorrow that eats away at my heart?

AARON   No, my lass, I can't say I've ever thought that.

AMULET   Well, then, let it pass, let it pass. My guilty shame
              shall stay closeted within my bosom. I shall drown
              my sorrow in the plying of my trade.

[Melody: "I'm Called Little Buttercup" from *H.M.S. Pinafore*]

> *I'm called Little Amulet, dear little Amulet*
> *Though I could never tell why.*
> *But still I'm called Amulet, dear little Amulet,*
> *Sweet little Amulet, I.*
>
> *I've flax and I've linen, and jars to put gin in*
> *Cartouches and ear-piercing knives*
> *Amphoras and scarabs, to sell to the Arabs*

To charm and inveigle their wives.

So, buy from dear Amulet, dear little Amulet
A bauble that catches your eye
A ring or a pendant, a bracelet resplendent
Oh, buy from dear Amulet, buy.

AARON We would be delighted to survey your wares, Amulet, but hark! Yonder comes the most noble of the Israelites! Fellow slaves, give heed to Moses!

MOSES My fellow Jews, good morning!

ALL Sir, good morning.

MOSES I hope you're all quite well.

ALL Quite well; and you, sir?

MOSES I am in reasonable health, for a man of eighty-four.

ALL You do us proud, sir!

[Melody: "Captain of the Pinafore" from *H.M.S. Pinafore*]

MOSES *I am the prophet of the Israelites*

ALL *And there's not another we would choose!*

MOSES *You're very, very good, and be it understood,*
You're a right fine bunch of Jews.

ALL *We're very, very good, and be it understood,*
We're a right fine bunch of Jews.

MOSES *Though my pedigree is lowly*
To posterity I'm holy
I'm devoted to my Hebrew flock,
And occasionally a rebel
Might make me smack a pebble,
But I'd never, never strike a rock!

ALL *What, never?*

MOSES	*No, never!*
ALL	*What, never?*
MOSES	*Well – hardly ever!*
ALL	*He'd hardly ever strike a rock!* *Then give a shrei to glorify* *The low-key prophet of the Israelites!* *Then give a shrei to glorify* *The prophet of the Israelites!*
MOSES	*I do my best to edify you all –*
ALL	*And to learn from you is our delight.*
MOSES	*You're the people of the book, and I'm glad I undertook* *To instruct you in wrong and right.*
ALL	*We're the people of the book, and he's glad he undertook* *To instruct us in wrong and right.*
MOSES	*To insolence and curse I'm thoroughly averse* *My lips abstain from speech that cuts –* *Though 'kakn oyfn yam' may on occasion drop there-* * from,* *You'll never hear me call you 'putz.'*
ALL	*What, never?*
MOSES	*No, never!*
ALL	*What, never?*
MOSES	*Well – hardly ever!*
ALL	*He will hardly ever call you 'putz'!* *Then give a shrei to glorify* *The well-bred prophet of the Israelites!* *Then give a shrei to glorify* *The prophet of the Israelites!*
AARON	Most esteemed leader, heed our cry. The oppression of our slavery plunges us into never-ending

unrest. We beg you to find us relief from our tangible despair.

MOSES   But, dear fellow Hebrew, how?

AARON   Perhaps you might approach the great Pharaoh himself, and appeal to his better nature.

MOSES   Mighty Pharaoh has no better nature. I fear that any such approach would engender disastrous consequences.

AARON   I believe you are quite mistaken, Moses. Pharaoh is a gentle and gracious monarch. It is his dreaded Grand Vizier, Titwillow, whose very presence instills terror and dismay.

MOSES   Now that you mention it, I have heard it said that the Pharaoh is no more than a well-intentioned nincompoop.

AARON   This may be an opportunity to discern the truth of that; for I see the Pharaoh himself approaches.

VIZIER   Make way, make way, for the Lord High Pharaoh!

AARON   Most supreme Majesty, we welcome you to our lowly work-yard.

MOSES   Mighty Pharaoh, it is a pleasure to greet you. We were just discussing your estimable virtues.

PHARAOH   The pleasure is entirely mine. It warms my heart to view such devoted and hardworking slaves, giving their all to improve their lot in life.

AARON   Is slavery indeed the path to advancement?

PHARAOH   It is. My own story is an example.

[Melody: "When I Was a Lad" from *H.M.S. Pinafore*]

When I was a lad, I scrubbed and swept

All the chambers of the palace of Amenhotept
I fed all the peacocks and I cleaned up the mess
And I polished up the sandals of the High Priestess

CHORUS   And he polished up the sandals of the High Priestess.

PHARAOH   I polished up her sandals so carefullee
              That now I am the Pharaoh of the dynasty!

CHORUS   He polished up her sandals so carefullee
              That now he is the Pharaoh of the dynasty.

PHARAOH   With brazen flummery and prudent bribes
              I rose to apprentice to the royal scribes
              While useless at the tasks that they perform,
              I could copy all the letters in cuneiform

CHORUS   He could copy all the letters in cuneiform.

PHARAOH   I copied those letters so officiously
              That now I am the Pharaoh of the dynasty!

CHORUS   He copied those letters so officiously
              That now he is the Pharaoh of the dynasty!

PHARAOH   By flattering employers without any shame
              An embalmer's assistant I soon became
              I brushed off the coffins and I dusted all the lids
              And sold tickets to the tourists at the Pyramids

CHORUS   He sold tickets to the tourists at the Pyramids!

PHARAOH   I sold so many tickets, they rewarded me
              By making me the Pharaoh of the dynasty!

CHORUS   He sold so many tickets they rewarded he
              By making him the Pharaoh of the dynasty!

PHARAOH   Now Egyptians all, wherever you may be
              If you want to rise to the top of the tree
              If you're widely known as a witless fool,
              Be careful to be guided by this golden rule.

CHORUS	*Be careful to be guided by this golden rule!*
PHARAOH	*Just butter up your betters, and I'll guarantee* *That you all may be Pharaohs of the dynasty!*
CHORUS	*Just butter up your betters, and he'll guarantee* *That you all may be Pharaohs of the dynasty!*
MOSES	It is indeed an inspiring tale of confident aspiration. Yet, despite this, honored Pharaoh, I needs must ask you to let my people go.
PHARAOH	To let your people go? What an absurd entreaty!
MOSES	It is the Israelites' fondest desire to go forth from Egypt and return to the land of our forbears.
PHARAOH	I beg you not to repeat this impertinent request. The slaves are here to make bricks of mud and straw, and make bricks they shall continue to do.
MOSES	A mightier ruler than thou shall bend your will, royal Pharaoh.
PHARAOH	Be still, vexatious Israelite! You begin to try my patience.
MOSES	Very well, I shall depart. But this matter is not yet concluded.
PHARAOH	How provoking this would be to a Pharaoh of less amiable disposition! I am surrounded by the most pestilential petitioners and aggravating adherents! Were I a vengeful monarch, they would suffer the most unpleasant sanctions.

[Melody: "As Someday It May Happen" from *The Mikado*]

As someday it may happen that a victim must be found
I've got a little list, I've got a little list
Of society offenders who might well be underground
And who never would be missed – who never would be
*   missed –*

> There's the icy-pawed embalmer with his creepy linen
> strips
> The vapid neo-pagan here to watch the full eclipse
> The repulsive Princess Cruisers from the Glory-of-the-
> Seas
> Who descend from their flotillas like a pack of hungry
> fleas
> And that pompous condescending snob, the Egyptolo-
> gist!
> They'd none of them be missed – they'd none of them be
> missed.

CHORUS   *He's got 'em on the list, he's got 'em on the list*
And they'd none of them be missed, they'd none of them
be missed.

PHARAOH   *And Napoleon's lieutenant who shot off the Sphinx's*
nose –
I've got him on the list – I've got him on the list.
The dunce who for the camera strikes a hieroglyphic pose
I've got him on the list – I've got him on the list
The nitwit who endeavors to defy the mummy's curse
The fool who scales a pyramid, and just to be perverse
The collector from a certain London national museum
Who filches every artifact from every mausoleum
And that blasted fellow Moses, Hebrew abolitionist!
He never would be missed – I'm sure he'd not be missed.

CHORUS   *He's got 'em on the list, he's got 'em on the list*
And he's sure they'd not be missed, he's sure they'd not
be missed.

VIZIER   Honored Pharaoh, the murmuring of the Israelite
slaves continues unabated. Have you any direc-
tives that might clarify for them their lowly destiny?

PHARAOH   Yes. Convey to the taskmasters that the slaves are
to double their quota of bricks, but must gather the
additional straw and mud themselves.

VIZIER   Very good, sir.

PHARAOH   But this instruction does not come from me, mind you. It is an order of the Grand Vizier, Titwillow.

VIZIER   Brilliant, sir. What an achievement, to have abstracted yourself from the most unpopular decisions.

PHARAOH   I agree. The invention of Titwillow has been an unqualified success. I even find myself, at times, believing in his existence.

VIZIER   He is indeed the most useful member of the royal court, insubstantial as he may be.

***

AARON   The Hebrews are suffering intolerably, Moses, under this supplemental oppression.

MOSES   Much as I despair to do so, it is my duty to unleash upon Pharaoh the full force of Divine wroth.

AARON   Has it come to that?

MOSES   Yes, I'm afraid it has. The Pharaoh must know a power beyond his own. With a wave of my shepherd's staff, I hereby impose upon Egypt the most terrifying and discomforting of afflictions!

[Melody: "Tree Little Maids" from *The Mikado*]

THE PLAGUES   *Ten little plagues from God are we*
Here to defy your Majesty
All in the cause of liberty
Ten little plagues from God!

Blood in the Nile will be number one,
Then with the frogs you'll be overrun,
Lice are the next phenomenon,
Ten little plagues from God!

Then comes a plague that's veterinary
Blight in amounts extraordinary

Boils that require an apothecary,
Ten little plagues from God!

Next to the hail will your crops succumb
Locusts will bring pandemonium
Darkness your nation will overcome
Ten little plagues from God!

If nine little plagues don't win the day,
Then you shall see what a price you'll pay
The tenth will, no doubt, all the rest outweigh
Ten little plagues from God,
Ten little plagues from God!

PHARAOH   Moses, I come to you in the most abject defeat. Your signs and wonders have conquered Egypt. We can countenance no more. Take your fellow Hebrews and depart to your ancestral land.

AMULET   Oh, joy! Rapture!

AARON   We shall make our preparations at once.

PHARAOH   And so the slaves shall leave Egypt. I cannot help but feel that part of me goes with them.

AMULET   Sublime king, your compassion moves me to confess the awful secret of my soul – for it concerns your royal self most intimately.

PHARAOH   I'm not certain that I want to hear it.

AMULET   But you must! And you, also, Moses, for I shall reveal the surprising story of your own noble birth.

MOSES   This has always been of great interest to me.

AMULET   Very well, then. Many years ago, I was maidservant to a Pharaoh's daughter. She was mother to a lovely baby boy, and it was my happy task to bathe this royal child each morning in the River Nile.

All was well until, one day, as I sat by the river's

edge, guarding the baby in his basket, I was momentarily distracted by a passing crocodile. I then turned back to my young charge, picked up the basket and took him back to his nursery in the palace.

It was not until later that day when I realized that this child was not the baby Pharaoh, but another child who had been floating in the Nile in a basket. I discovered that the little boy was not an Egyptian, but, in fact, a Hebrew infant.

PHARAOH   How could you tell?

AMULET   There are ways to discern. Ever since that fateful day, my spirit has been burdened by this awful secret, and I have ached to know what became of that royal infant that I so shamefully failed to safeguard.

MOSES   Amulet, he stands before you this moment!

AMULET   (*gasps*) Are you he?

MOSES   I am. It has long been my family's legend that, having been launched down the Nile in a pitch-lined basket, I floated back to my parents when the river's tide reversed. Yet your surprising tale suggests that this was not the case.

AARON   And what of the Hebrew baby?

PHARAOH   As scandalous as it may seem, *I* was that Hebrew baby.

MOSES   What an unexpected turn of events.

PHARAOH   Indeed it is. The royal court has frequently noted my lack of resemblance to my mummified family. I had attributed this anomaly to my complete set of internal organs; but this revelation explains it much more reasonably.

VIZIER   But, Pharaoh, this means you're one of the He-
               brews!

AARON   And, Moses, likewise it indicates that *you* are of
               royal Egyptian blood!

AMULET   Are you angry at your poor little Amulet, Moses?

MOSES   Be assured that I am not. Despite my royal birth, I
               feel at one with the Hebrews who raised me to the
               highest station within their ranks.

PHARAOH   And I now have a satisfactory explanation for my
               kindly feelings toward the slaves.

VIZIER   But what's to happen next? Will the Hebrews go
               free? If so, in what company?

MOSES   I insist that the Hebrews shall depart Egypt at their
               convenience.

PHARAOH   And I likewise so insist. With myself as their es-
               cort.

VIZIER   I know of one luminary who won't be pleased.

MOSES   And who may that be?

VIZIER   The Grand Vizier Titwillow.

PHARAOH   The Grand Vizier no longer presents an obstacle.
               Allow me to tell you of Titwillow's fate.

[Melody: "Titwillow" from *The Mikado*]

> *On the bank of the ocean a chamberlain sits,*
> *Name of Willow, Titwillow, Titwillow;*
> *As majestically as his condition permits*
> *O Willow, Titwillow, Titwillow.*
> *"Do you mourn the escape of the Hebrews," I said,*
> *"Or the anguish to which your perversity led?*
> *Do you wish you had never arisen from bed?*
> *Oh, Willow, Titwillow, Titwillow."*

He scowled and he snarled as he sat on that bank,
Singing Willow, Titwillow, Titwillow.
With a sneering expression befitting his rank
O Willow, Titwillow, Titwillow.
And he said, as his last inhalation he drew,
"Not a stroke of the whip on a slave do I rue
But to think of my empire outdone by a Jew!"
O Willow, Titwillow, Titwillow.

Then this obdurate chamberlain took off his socks
Titwillow, Titwillow, Titwillow.
And his surplice's pockets he loaded with rocks
O Willow, Titwillow, Titwillow.
Then some anti-Semitic invective he gave
And he plunged himself into the billowy wave
And 'tis thus the Red Sea is the autocrat's grave –
O Willow, Titwillow, Titwillow.

AMULET   Why, then, the despot is no more, and the Hebrews' liberation has come!

CHORUS   Hurrah, hurrah!

AARON   Not only that, but an infant Israelite has led us to victory and been returned to his people!

CHORUS   Hurrah, hurrah!

PHARAOH   And the Pharaoh of Egypt has turned away from tyranny and pledged himself to righteousness.

AARON   For he is an Israelite!

[Melody: "He Is an Englishman" from *H.M.S. Pinafore*]

MOSES   *He is an Israelite!*
Though it stunned a Pharaoh's scion
To become a son of Zion
Yet he is an Israelite,

CHORUS   *Yet he is an Israelite!*

MOSES   *For he might have been a Canaanite*
                 A Phoenician or an Amorite
                 Or perhaps Samaritan!

CHORUS   *Or perhaps Samaritan!*

                 For in spite of all temptation
                 To be Philistine or Thracian,
                 He remains an Israelite,
                 He remains an I-i-i-i-i-i-i-israelite!

                 Hurrah! Hurrah! Hurrah!

La Forza del Dayenu

— an Italian opera —

The Exodus story is very dramatic, and Italian opera is likewise very dramatic.

That's it. That's all I've got.

One thing I learned while writing these lyrics, is why Italian opera is written in Italian (besides the fact that the librettists lived in Italy). Italian *always* sounds good. When you hear Italians, they seem to be singing even if they're not. It has so many vowels. English, on the other hand, is choppy and almost all the syllables are divided by consonants. So writing, not to mention singing, words to very lyrical melodies in English is a challenge.

But that was *my* challenge; I think you have a bigger one, should you decide to include this shpiel in your seder. Your singers have to know the melodies quite well, and, since there's no musical notation here, assess how the lines scan. I've put in the right number of syllables, but you have to match them to the music.

And it's undeniable that arias sound better with accompaniment. You need to decide how to deal with this. It occurred to me that the way to go might be the Victor Café way. In Philadelphia, there's an opera restaurant where all the waiters are voice students in professional training. Frequently, you'll hear a bell ring in the dining room, and one of the wait-staff begins to sing accompanied by a recording. If you'd like to do that, you could create a playlist and rig up the music in or near the dining room. For the dialogue, I think, you'll need to improvise *recitativo secco*.

Before you waste any time looking for profundity in this shpiel, be advised that it's just for fun. It's mostly about eating and drinking, anyhow.

And if you really choose to perform this one, all I can say is: better you than I.

191

CHORUS
ALFREDO
VIOLETTA
MUSETTA
THE DUKE (OF MANTUA)
LIONEL

[Melody: "Va pensiero" from Verdi's *Nabucco*]

CHORUS

Now the springtime again warms our shivering souls
Sleepy blossoms the gentle sun caresses
Our reunion the new season blesses
Loving faces round our table light our hearts.
Candle-light, glimmering bright, opens the holiday
Here at home, may the seder bring joyous satiety.
And our voices, together in harmony
Tell the next generation the tale our past imparts.

Now, recline, pour the wine, as we recall burdens we
*   bore*
In a land of affliction and heartache
From on high, Adonai led us through sea, safely ashore
a supreme, holy pact to undertake
Though in bondage we this year travail,
In the next, may we be in Israel.
Our reunion the new season blesses
Loving faces round our table light our hearts.
Round the table, your faces light our hearts.
Round the table, your faces light our hearts.

ALFREDO

Welcome, beloved friends and family! We are so happy to see you once again at our seder table.

LIONEL

Your lovely home always puts everyone in a festive mood.

THE DUKE

Not to mention Violetta's wonderful cooking!

ALFREDO

All in good time, Duke. We've lit the candles, and it's time to recite the Kiddush. Everyone, raise your glasses!

[Melody: "Libiam" from Verdi's *La Traviata*]

ALFREDO   *We drink, and we toast with the fruit of the vine,*
to remember our liberation from servitude
We bless Adonai, and we warble our gratitude
Not to be in bondage anymore.
Enjoined to indulge in four glasses,
We really should do this more often.
Boray p'ree ha-gafen,
And then we greet Elijah at the door –
We drink, and we're holy, we're holy with mitsvas
Rememb'ring the great redemption of yore.

CHORUS   *And we remember the redemption of yore,*
And we remember the redemption of yore.

VIOLETTA   *Take care, as you gleefully sample the wine,*
To avoid spilling any vintage on the tablecloth
It's rude and uncivil to act like a Visigoth
This took a week to prepare.

I sold all our pasta and bagels
And stashed the hametsdiche dishes
I cooked and I stuffed two gefilte fishes
This must be a very kosher affair –
So drink, and be holy, be holy with mitsvas
And don't pass over one solitary prayer!

CHORUS   *We drink, and we toast with the fruit of the vine,*
to remember our liberation from servitude
We bless Adonai, and we warble our gratitude
Not to be in bondage anymore.

ALFREDO   *You always set such a fine table*

VIOLETTA   *Of course, for a day that's so holy*

ALFREDO   *I can't wait to taste that ravioli*

VIOLETTA   *Sometimes, you really drive me to despair –*

CHORUS   *We drink, and we toast with the fruit of the vine,*

> *To remember our liberation from servitude*
> *We bless Adonai, and we warble our gratitude*
> *Not to be in bondage anymore.*
> *Not in chains anymore,*
> *Not in chains anymore,*
> *So drink and bless and sing and eat tonight!*

VIOLETTA   Wonderful, dear friends! Now we wash our hands, dip a vegetable in salt water, and invite all who are hungry to come and eat.

THE DUKE   I'm *very* hungry.

VIOLETTA   Well, to eat a little later. First we present the un-leavened bread – the matza, bread of affliction. We take the middle sheet, break it in half …

MUSETTA   And hide the bigger half!

VIOLETTA   *(laughs)* That's right, Musetta, we hide it to keep it safe. We can't finish the seder without it!

MUSETTA   It's not safe from *me!*

ALFREDO   Before we think about the afikomen, Musetta – don't you have some questions you'd like to ask?

MUSETTA   Yes, I do.

[Melody: "Musetta's Waltz" from Puccini's *La Boheme*]

MUSETTA   *Why is this night, so unlike all the rest of the nights,*
So remote from normality?
Why have we matza here, in the place of foccacia, pita,
*   Kaiser rolls and naan?*
Last night, we had just normal vegetables, they're really
*   nothing special –*
But on this night, we face the bitterest, most incendiary
*   herb.*
We never dip in salty water, because, why should we?
But this night, not once but, two times we dip parsley.

> *All other nights, we eat either reclining, or sitting up if*
> *we choose to —*
> *But now we all recline, on a pillow as liberated children*
> *of Israel do!*

LIONEL   Well done, Musetta!

MUSETTA   Thank you very much.

THE DUKE   Did it take you a long time to learn the four questions?

MUSETTA   Oh, no, it was easy. I've been singing it as I walk down the street. Everybody looks at me, but I know it's because they're jealous.

VIOLETTA   Of course they are, my lovely child. Now, let's answer the questions by telling the Exodus story.

LIONEL   There arose a new king in Egypt who knew not Joseph. And he feared the people of Israel, saying, "These people are too numerous for us; if we go to war, they may join with our enemies!"

ALFREDO   And so the Pharaoh enslaved our ancestors and set them to making bricks of straw and mud. They were forced to build the store-cities of Pithom and Ramses.

VIOLETTA   And then, Pharaoh decreed that all the firstborn boys be thrown into the Nile!

THE DUKE   A Hebrew family from the Levite tribe sent their newborn son floating down the Nile in a pitch-lined basket. And the baby was found by the Pharaoh's daughter, who adopted him, named him Moses, and raised him in the palace.

VIOLETTA   But, after Moses grew to manhood, he defended a Hebrew slave who was being beaten. He slew the slave's attacker, and fled to the land of Midian.

LIONEL   There he became a shepherd, and one day Moses saw a bush that was burning, but ...

MUSETTA   But it wasn't burning up. We already know this story!

THE DUKE   And we're so hungry!

LIONEL   And dinner smells so good!

[Melody: "Anvil Chorus" from Verdi's *Il Trovatore*]

CHORUS   *Sitting and reading and singing and waiting and starving with nothing but matza and parsley!*
Smelling the chicken, the soup, and the brisket, my insides rebel and my patience departs me!
When's dinner? When's dinner?
Hey! Have mercy!
Bring out the food before I die of malnutrition!
Feed me or I shall undergo decomposition!
Yes – yes – yes – I can wait no more.
The seder's too long – can't sing one more song – give me some sustenance!

Forty more pages, I'm chewing my napkin, and now the maror starts to look tempting to me!
Dayenu, dayenu!
How do the other guests not hear my growling tummy?
Maybe the seder plate should be protected from me!
Let's – all – say – Motsi le<u>h</u>em, please!
This recitation – is a vexation – let's have some chow – right now!

THE DUKE   Everyone, I believe I know how to speed up this seder.

MUSETTA   You do? How?

THE DUKE   Just listen to this.

[Melody: "La donna e mobile" from Verdi's *Rigoletto*]

THE DUKE   *Wash your hands in the sink*

Then you can have a drink
Horseradish, it's been said,
Surely will clear your head
Chew on a matza sheet
Tastes just like concrete
Pass the salt-water bowl
It's seder protocol.

Once again we gotta
Listen to my fadda
Reading the haggadah
Serve us the meal!

Gefilte-fish on the plates
Always coagulates
Give me a matza-ball
It's so Levitical
While you eat brisket
Wishing for a biscuit
I've afikomen
In my abdomen

Some believe haroses
Gives you halitosis
Had enough of Moses?
See you next year!
See you next year!

ALFREDO   That was brilliant, Duke!

THE DUKE   Thank you, Alfredo, you're very kind.

ALFREDO   Violetta, please have some more horseradish – it will cure what ails you.

VIOLETTA   Thanks. Still, it's sad to think that the seder's all over.

LIONEL   But the most important part of Passover isn't even tonight. It's tomorrow!

MUSETTA   Tomorrow? What happens tomorrow?

LIONEL   The most glorious event of the entire year!

[Melody: "M'appari" from Flotow's *Marta*]

LIONEL   *Matza brei – that's what I adore,*
                With a pile of it, I'll always ask for more
                Just a dry overture to crumbs,
                Ambrosia it soon becomes.

                Amateur epicure, you'll need nothing else all week
                Even when pantry shelves seem discouraging and bleak
                Get a pan, get some eggs, put a kettle on to boil,
                And an onion, a strainer, and pepper, and margarine, or
                        olive oil –

                Matza brei, salted and serene
                Amber-brown, how you crown Ashkenaz cuisine.
                Tell my mom I will not allow her
                To make me eat potato flour.

CHORUS   *Matza, matza, to the feast we*
                Come pajama'd down the stair
                A week of privation, but at least we
                Nosh on angels' breakfast fare –
                Ah, we nosh on holy angels' fare!

Let My People Free-Associate

— a session with Sigmund Freud —

Why is this *shpiel* different from all the other *shpiels?*

First, there are only two roles, except for a brief appearance of a secretary on the first page. Next, the play is less humorous and more academic. Third, its scope is theological, not specifically Exodus-oriented, although it mentions the seder.

The Jewishness of Sigmund Freud, and his psychoanalytic approach to religions including Judaism, have been discussed for many decades. Those are worth exploring. But in this brief play, I tried to expose aspects of the connection between Freudian analysis and the rational religious philosophy of Rabbi Mordecai M. Kaplan.

Rabbi Kaplan, who founded the Reconstructionist Jewish denomination, defined Judaism as an evolving religious civilization. The constant throughout Jewish history, he wrote, is the Jewish people: not God, Who has been envisioned by Jews in a variety of ways for thousands of years.

So, since I am a Reconstructionist rabbi, I imagined an anxious Jewish everyman, plagued by doubts about an anthropomorphic God-idea, on the couch of a Reconstructionist therapist. Since Kaplan's philosophy is so well grounded in psychology and sociology, and so convincingly logical, I decided to name that therapist Sigmund Freud. And I feel that neither the rabbi nor the doctor would be displeased with the result.

DR. FREUD
(JOSEPH) ISRAEL
SECRETARY

DR. FREUD   How much time have I until his appointment?

SECRETARY   Just five minutes, Dr. Freud. And you haven't recorded your notes from his last session.

DR. FREUD   I'll have to look at my notebook then. But it's hard to read my handwriting. Could you try, please?

SECRETARY   Certainly, Doctor. "Mr. Joseph Israel. The patient presents with an unusual set of symptoms, including repetitive prayer rituals, recurrent thoughts of persecution, and a persistent sense of guilt centering upon his father.

"Mr. Israel also exhibits a delusional tendency. At times he says that his father is Abraham, the Biblical patriarch; at other times he recalls being the son of a suburban Jewish family in northern New Jersey. He described a dream in which his father was pursuing him with a knife, and tying him to an altar. He is tortured by conflicting feelings of loving and resenting his mother. Constantly he is afraid of disappointing the expectations of others."

DR. FREUD   Thank you, Miss Slip. I don't know what I'd do without you.

SECRETARY   Here's something else you scribbled at the bottom: "Mr. Israel expresses anxiety about the upcoming Passover seder. He feels guilt about repeating as truth a story he does not believe, yet wishes to avoid conflict with his family."

DR. FREUD   A very interesting case.

SECRETARY   Oh, here he is now. Shall I send him in?

DR. FREUD   Yes, please do. Good morning, Mr. Israel.

ISRAEL   Good morning, Dr. Freud.

DR. FREUD   Let me shut the door. Please have a seat on the couch, or lie down if you prefer.

ISRAEL   Okay.

DR. FREUD   Mr. Israel, looking over my notes of our last session, I am intrigued by the habit you told me about – saying the same prayers over and over, sometimes every day, and the repetitive rituals you feel you must perform. Would you tell me a little more about those, please?

ISRAEL   Well, I say the Sh'ma every day, at least. I go to the synagogue every week.

DR. FREUD   What is the Sh'ma?

ISRAEL   Sh'ma Yisrael, Adonai elohaynu, Adonai e̲had. It means, Hear, Israel, Adonai is our God, Adonai is one.

DR. FREUD   Tell me about Adonai.

ISRAEL   Well, Adonai is the Creator. Adonai made all the rules. And judges our behavior, and decides our fate, and gives us everything we need. Adonai is – Adonai is everything. You know, everywhere. In charge.

DR. FREUD   And therefore you must say every day that Adonai is God, so that Adonai will judge you favorably?

ISRAEL   Not just that. It's also – not eating pork, and touching the mezuza when you come into the house, and fasting on Yom Kippur.

DR. FREUD   What would happen if you didn't do these things?

ISRAEL   Oh – it would be terrible!

DR. FREUD   Why? What would happen?

ISRAEL   God would be angry, and my parents would be disappointed … I would feel awful. Like a failure. I should be a good Jew.

DR. FREUD   How do you know God would be angry with you?

ISRAEL   You know, the Prophets are always saying, like, "Woe to the wicked, it shall be ill with him." And all those punishments in the Bible – one guy was struck dead just for collecting manna on Shabbat – when God gets angry, it's not good.

DR. FREUD   Adonai seems very angry. So, Mr. Israel, what do you think of Adonai?

ISRAEL   What do you mean, what do I think? It doesn't matter what I think, I just have to *do* all this stuff.

DR. FREUD   It matters to *me* what you think.

ISRAEL   Well, then I guess I … I wish God would just back off sometimes.

DR. FREUD   What would be different then?

ISRAEL   I guess I could just be a good Jew my own way.

DR. FREUD   Can you remember a time when you didn't feel that Adonai was so angry?

ISRAEL   Sure! But it was a very long time ago.

DR. FREUD   Tell me about it.

ISRAEL   I was very little. It was in a garden … a long time before …

DR. FREUD   Before what?

ISRAEL   Before all those punishments.

DR. FREUD   Why were you punished?

ISRAEL	I can't remember.
DR. FREUD	It sounds like something very important happened. If you are able to remember it, then you can deal with it out in the open, and come to some resolution.
ISRAEL	I don't want to. It's too terrible to remember.
DR. FREUD	The memory is buried in your unconscious. But you cannot allow it to remain there, because this repressed memory is still causing you great distress.
ISRAEL	But what can I do about it?
DR. FREUD	Why don't we just have a talk. You say whatever comes into your head, even if it doesn't make any sense. You don't have to be embarrassed, because I'm your doctor and will never tell anyone.
ISRAEL	I'll try it, if you think it will help.
DR. FREUD	All right then. Relax and just say the first thing you think of. I'll start by saying ... sheep.
ISRAEL	Sacrifice.
DR. FREUD	Father.
ISRAEL	Sacrifice.
DR. FREUD	God.
ISRAEL	Sacrifice.
DR. FREUD	Well, then, let me say ... sacrifice.
ISRAEL	Stop it!
DR. FREUD	Does this cause you distress?
ISRAEL	Yes, but, I was saying, the first thing that comes into my head is, stop it.

DR. FREUD   Who should stop it?

ISRAEL   My father should stop it. No … no, not my father. He was just doing what Adonai told him to do.

DR. FREUD   And what did Adonai tell your father to do?

ISRAEL   To sacrifice me.

DR. FREUD   You? To sacrifice you?

ISRAEL   Yes. To tie me to an altar and sacrifice me as a gift to God. That's what my father started to do.

DR. FREUD   But obviously, he didn't sacrifice you. You are here.

ISRAEL   *(louder)* Yes, I'm here! Scarred for life, but I'm here!

DR. FREUD   It sounds like you are very angry at your father.

ISRAEL   I'm sort of angry at him … but not really. He was doing what God told him to do. My father was kind of a nebbish. He couldn't say no. Well, almost never – he certainly argued with Adonai about Sodom and Gomorrah. But he was a wimp. I feel sorry for him.

DR. FREUD   Nonetheless, you are angry.

ISRAEL   I'm – I – I think I'm angry at God.

DR. FREUD   Ah. You're angry at God. And that's something very bad, you feel? You should be punished for this?

ISRAEL   Well – I don't know, really. I'm very conflicted about this. I think I try as hard as the next guy to be a good person. But, getting angry at God – that's going too far. That's asking for trouble.

DR. FREUD   Do you feel your punishments were just?

ISRAEL   They were all just. I deserved them, and more.

DR. FREUD   For what offense?

ISRAEL   For being a bad Jew. I've done lots of bad things.
                Like, I rebelled against Moses. And there were all
                the times I worshipped idols. Also I had a shrimp
                cocktail at a party once.

DR. FREUD   It sounds as if you feel very guilty.

ISRAEL   Yes, I do. It keeps me up at night sometimes.

DR. FREUD   I see what you mean about your conflict. You try
                to be a good person, but you feel you've done
                many bad things. You think you deserve to be
                punished, and yet you're angry at God for punish-
                ing you.

ISRAEL   There's one thing I'm sure of: I *am* a moral person.
                I am committed to making the world a better place,
                and treating my neighbor as I want to be treated. I
                know I backslide sometimes, but, you know, I'm
                still trying.

DR. FREUD   Let's talk about your father some more. What was
                he like? What do you remember about him?

ISRAEL   Oh, he was a great man. The founder of the Jewish
                people, after all! He was very powerful, and wise,
                and he spoke with God personally. He always
                knew where we were going and what we were
                supposed to do.

DR. FREUD   Did he protect you? Did he make you feel safe?

ISRAEL   I *used* to feel safe. But then it changed.

DR. FREUD   In what way?

ISRAEL   Well, that time with the sacrifice, that was pretty
                horrible. After that I began to think that maybe he
                wasn't always looking out for me. In fact, there
                was another time he came after me with a knife,
                too, and I was terrified. But it turned out he was

only going to circumcise me. Still, I had night-mares.

DR. FREUD   Did you think of him as all-powerful?

ISRAEL   I used to. He really could do a lot of things. He destroyed the idols in my grandfather's shop because they were an abomination. That took a lot of guts. And he led the whole tribe to the Promised Land. But then when I saw he couldn't save the city of Sodom, I began to have my doubts.

DR. FREUD   And did this make you feel worried?

ISRAEL   Worried, yes, and scared. The world isn't such a friendly place, you know. And if cities are going to get destroyed and people are going to get sacrificed, and my dad doesn't stop it, then what's going to happen to *me?* I'm no big hero. If some army comes at me with chariots, I have no idea what to do. Run, maybe.

DR. FREUD   And this makes you feel anxious.

ISRAEL   Sure.

DR. FREUD   So, tell me a little bit about Adonai. Or, excuse me, is it God?

ISRAEL   It depends what language you're speaking. Adonai is Hebrew.

DR. FREUD   Go on.

ISRAEL   Adonai is all-knowing. Adonai is infinite, and just, and merciful, and created all the rules about being good. Elohaynu mele<u>h</u> ha-olam, after all.

DR. FREUD   What's the relationship between the two of you?

ISRAEL   If I do what Adonai wants me to, I'll be okay. For example, if I don't work on Shabbat, and if I say Kaddish for my parents, and give charity, and stay faithful to my wife, and throw pieces of bread in the water on Rosh Hashana.

DR. FREUD   Then you will be okay.

ISRAEL   Yes.

DR. FREUD   And how does it make you feel to do those things?

ISRAEL   I feel much happier. Relaxed, less worried. Relieved, I guess, is the word.

DR. FREUD   Do you feel that, if you faithfully do all these things, Adonai will protect you?

ISRAEL   Sure. That's the deal! The covenant, you know. I walk in God's way, and God will return my faithfulness. It's all in the Torah.

DR. FREUD   In what way would God protect you? Protect you from what?

ISRAEL   From – from bad things happening. I'll have a good life. Like, for *sure* I wouldn't get sacrificed.

DR. FREUD   So, Mr. Israel, let me ask you this. Do you know other people who do all these things, keep kosher, say the prayers, et cetera?

ISRAEL   Of course. Thousands of people do those things. They have for centuries!

DR. FREUD   And do they all have good lives as a consequence?

ISRAEL   Uh – it's – it's hard to say. I guess not all of them do.

DR. FREUD   Didn't many of them perish at the hands of the Nazis?

ISRAEL   *(pause)* I guess they did.

DR. FREUD   So perhaps we may posit that this covenant is not objective reality.

ISRAEL   Well, it doesn't turn out the way it's been written.
              But are you saying that it's all a fake?

DR. FREUD   No, no, Mr. Israel, I'm not saying that at all. This
              covenant is serving a vital purpose. You said it
              yourself.

ISRAEL   I said what?

DR. FREUD   You said that these rituals make you feel happier,
              relieved, more relaxed. That, instead of having ter-
              ror and sleepless nights, you can function in soci-
              ety. This is not an insubstantial thing.

ISRAEL   You make it sound like I'm nuts.

DR. FREUD   Not at all. It is merely a coping mechanism. A
              strategy used by an individual to ward off the
              anxiety caused by separation from the father.

ISRAEL   What does my father have to do with it?

DR. FREUD   Mr. Israel, when you were a child, you believed
              your father, and your mother too, were all-
              powerful. All children believe that. If they did not,
              they would be so constantly fearful of the universe,
              that they could not possibly focus on learning to
              function in it.

              But at a certain point you, just like everyone, found
              that your father was not all just, all good, omnipo-
              tent. He could not protect you from everything. In
              fact, as you grew up, you even noticed that you
              were as big as he – he, the immense guardian of
              your world! Naturally this produced anxiety, and
              a healthy person seeks to relieve anxiety. This you
              have done. You have replaced your fallible father
              with an infallible one; and it makes you relieved
              and tranquil. We call this 'transference.'

ISRAEL   But the problem is, now I feel like an idiot – like
              I've been talking to someone who isn't there. The

big guy who spoke through the burning bush, split the Red Sea, sent the ten plagues – this is a huge part of my world. I've repeated it so many times, and my children sit there, chewing on parsley, listening to me. Now you're saying God is something I've invented so I can feel better? How can I participate in a seder anymore? How can I go to services?

DR. FREUD   Mr. Israel, do you consider yourself a rational man?

ISRAEL   What do you mean?

DR. FREUD   Do you believe that what is true can be determined by observation, by experience? That a proposed truth can be tested, and if it's not supported by evidence, must be discarded? In other words, do you subscribe to science?

ISRAEL   Of course I do. I'm a modern person.

DR. FREUD   And what is the purpose of scientific study?

ISRAEL   To find the order in the universe – unity.

DR. FREUD   So we pursue our scientific studies because of our own, subjective need for order and unity.

ISRAEL   You could say that. The world would still go on if we didn't study it, but we still feel the urge to study it.

DR. FREUD   And we have no proof that the picture of the universe that has been constructed by scientists, is truly its actual nature. Any day we may be confronted with another Copernicus, another Galileo, and we will have to revise all our scientific truths.

ISRAEL   But we still have to keep trying to understand. We have to have faith in the rationality of the world's structure.

DR. FREUD   Exactly. To lose that faith would be skepticism – a surrender to unreason. So let us examine your problem more deeply. We are able to identify the factors that influence your idea of God: your fear of the dangers surrounding you, your longing for a replacement for your protective parents, and your need for a clear meaning in your life. These factors describe only your need for God – not the nature of God.

ISRAEL   I have non-religious friends who can't believe dogma. They say it's supported only by hearsay, not objective observations. They say that religion is all about submission to authority.

DR. FREUD   But they confuse religious doctrine with religion. Perhaps there is an element of authority in traditional religion, but not long ago, authority was important in science too. That changed because our approach to science changed – it improved, I think. Is this not also true of Judaism? Can one fairly accuse God of non-existence because of our faulty reasoning?

ISRAEL   But if God isn't the authority, then what's the alternative? God's just an ancient belief of primitive people? Where does that leave *me?*

DR. FREUD   My dear Mr. Israel, your people's idea of God has been changing for millennia. If you could put the prophet Moses in a room with the medieval philosopher Maimonides, Maimonides would consider Moses a primitive, and Moses would think Maimonides was an atheist. They had different beliefs about the nature of God, because they lived in different times, and philosophy evolves. Would you argue that Moses was not a Jew?

ISRAEL   No, of course not.

DR. FREUD   Or Maimonides?

ISRAEL   He was our greatest philosopher.

DR. FREUD   The Passover seder, I think, is the essential expression of Jewish communal life. You sit with your family and friends, you enjoy the food, you perform the rituals, you discuss philosophy. Let's be specific. When you read the story of the enslavement in Egypt and the Exodus, Mr. Israel, what impression do you get of Adonai?

ISRAEL   Ah ... well, Adonai speaks to Moses out of the burning bush, sends Moses and Aaron to Pharaoh to free the slaves, inflicts the ten plagues on Egypt. I'd say that leaves an impression of a very powerful, determined, pissed-off God.

DR. FREUD   A God who turned the Nile River, which is sacred to the Egyptians, to blood. A God who blots out the sun with the plague of darkness ... the sun, which the Egyptians also venerated. A God who frees slaves. The most important thing is not what God *is like*, but how God *functions*.

ISRAEL   I can see you're trying to get at something.

DR. FREUD   Mr. Israel, in the Bible you read the sacred memories of your ancestors. It's true that the images they recorded are mythic – they portrayed God as a "man of war," for instance – but, in this particular story, they described a force that works through humanity to resist tyrants. A power that inspires Moses to free the slaves. The function of this God is to make human efforts significant. This is an enormously important part of the universe, especially as we try to make sense of our role in it.

ISRAEL   You sound like that Hassidic rabbi – Menachem somebody –

DR. FREUD   Menachem Mendel of Kotsk.

ISRAEL   Yes. "God lives where we let God in."

DR. FREUD   And this doesn't sound very much like a punishing parent, does it?

ISRAEL No, but in those Bible stories, He sure was.

DR. FREUD The Bible was a product of its time. Your ancestors were searching for the Divine, and they described it in physical terms, the only way they knew. But if you search their words, if you analyze them, you discern a pattern. Their God commanded holiness. Holiness was achieved by living a moral life and creating a just society.

ISRAEL But those crazy random rules ...

DR. FREUD You cannot expect people to remove themselves from their cultural context. Those random rules were fairly unremarkable in the ancient Near East. And some were quite noble, at least in their intent. Rituals to demonstrate the sacredness of time ... rules that were reminders of the sanctity of family connections ... some a little awkward, perhaps, for our time, but still powerful and worth examination.

ISRAEL All right, so God commanded holiness. There was still a thinking, feeling, acting God who commanded. A personal God. There's no way around that. God talked to all those people, created miracles and all ...

DR. FREUD That was what the Biblical writers described. That was how they thought. But they did something much greater than this. They created an ethical religion: a system where a moral life was Divine service. Certainly there were sacrifices and hosannas; this was their super-ego finding a socially appropriate way to function. But, more important, they realized that their obligation was to repair the world, and they called this obligation God.

ISRAEL All the great religions have their Golden Rule.

DR. FREUD But the Hebrews were the first to see morality as divine. Think of the ancient Greeks and Romans. Did their gods command men to lead ethical lives?

ISRAEL   Their gods weren't very good ethical role models themselves.

DR. FREUD   And that is my point. The thing that causes you to repress your id for the good of society – to act altruistically, often against your own interest – that force is God. This is a constant through Jewish history, no matter how you choose to describe it.

ISRAEL   I can see that's what God has always done. But it's so hard to leave behind the traditional God. I think I really need an authority figure. It's comforting. I'm not sure that just having a force to connect with, is good enough. I can't talk to it.

DR. FREUD   In this, I fear I cannot help you. One of the goals of psychoanalysis is to free the patient from oppressive authority – especially that which he imposes on himself. Your comfort and security ultimately are your own responsibility. That's the price of being a grown-up. In fact, it can be argued that resisting the temptation to place one's decisions into the hands of another, is the only hope for civilization. Otherwise, the end of the road is fascism.

ISRAEL   Comparing traditional God-belief to fascism is pretty extreme, wouldn't you say, Doctor?

DR. FREUD   I don't compare them. I only say that, without the ability to take responsibility for our own lives, humanity is destined for nothing but fascism and fundamentalism.

ISRAEL   What about the Jews? They're my people and I love them, whether they believe the Bible literally or they're atheists. They're funny and they're great and they understand me.

DR. FREUD   What about them?

ISRAEL   What the heck are they *doing?* Why do we have a
              seder at all? Why celebrate any of the holidays, or
              get married under a huppah? If God didn't tell us
              to do it, then why do it?

DR. FREUD   Because they are the vehicles in which we carry our
              values. Because they are the way we have the great
              conversation. It's how we encounter the eternal
              questions. We live through ritual and through sto-
              ries, and together we try to work out how to repair
              this broken world. Let me ask you – at your bar
              mitsva, didn't the rabbi say, "Judaism cannot offer
              you answers; all it offers is a conversation"?

ISRAEL   No, he didn't.

DR. FREUD   Well, he should have. Mr. Israel, our people have
              done something ingenious, something no other an-
              cient people could do. They have taken the super-
              ego, the force of our ideals, our conscience, and
              lifted it up to the level of divinity. They desire so
              much that we should control our id, our need for
              self-gratification. They want to protect the weaker
              members of society. They want to make this world
              into the Garden of Eden. They desire this so much
              that they called this great desire God, and taught us
              to obey it at all cost.

ISRAEL   And now we spend all our time trying to figure out
              how.

DR. FREUD   Yes, exactly. We, and every generation before us.
              And, I hope, after us. That is the great conversa-
              tion. And since we know the vocabulary, we un-
              derstand the references, we share the assumptions
              – we converse in a Jewish context.

ISRAEL   I think I see. So it's not really disloyal to argue
              about God; it's actually sort of a commandment.
              Dr. Freud, I notice that you started to refer to "we
              Jews." Is it possible that you, yourself, still identify
              with the Jewish people? Are all *your* questions part

of the great conversation?

DR. FREUD   *Ach, tayer, a brokhe oyf dein kop.*[1]

ISRAEL   I guess my time's up. I hope you have a happy Passover, Doctor.

DR. FREUD   *A zisser Pesah, mein freund.*[2]

---

[1] "Ah, my dear one, a blessing on your head."
[2] "A sweet Passover, my friend."

ABOUT THE AUTHOR

Rabbi Shoshana Hantman grew up in the West Mount Airy section of Philadelphia, and was educated at Gratz College and the University of Pennsylvania. She received ordination from the Reconstructionist Rabbinical College, and a master's degree in education from Temple University. Shoshana has served as both a congregational rabbi and a synagogue education director; in 1992, she founded, and still directs, the independent Halutsim Hebrew School, where the students read plays in class nearly every week. Shoshana lives in northern Westchester County, New York, with her husband Richard Weill and their two children. *Passover Parodies* is her first book.